CONSCIOUS
EMPOWERMENT

CONSCIOUS EMPOWERMENT

A GUIDE TO HELPING GIRLS BUILD SELF-ESTEEM & CONFIDENCE

LEAH BERDYSZ, MSSA, LSW

NEW DEGREE PRESS

CONSCIOUS EMPOWERMENT

A Guide to Helping Girls Build Self-Esteem & Confidence

ISBN   978-1-63676-865-6   *Paperback*

978-1-63730-177-7   *Kindle Ebook*

978-1-63730-309-2   *Ebook*

CONTENTS

——

*This book is dedicated to girls from all backgrounds
and to the rock star parents, caregivers, and role models
helping them grow into strong, confident women.
You matter. You are loved. And you are enough.*

INTRODUCTION

———

Being vulnerable is hard. Being someone you're not is harder.

Even though I deeply value speaking my truth, sometimes it can be extremely challenging. Writing this book was hard. Speaking about my mental health challenges was hard. Asking people to support this book was hard.

I was scared to write this book. I often asked myself, "Who am I to tell others how they can help raise girls to be strong, resilient, and confident when these are all things I struggle with myself?" I don't have my own children. I am still learning.

Then I realized, over the past six years of helping others grow stronger, I've grown stronger. Educating over seven hundred students in social–emotional skills over a few years took self-empowerment. Becoming an entrepreneur required faith in myself. Going back to school took confidence. Being vulnerable enough to learn about people different than myself took courage.

Daring to dream of a better world for girls to live in requires bravery. Reaching out to countless individuals to take part in this process demonstrates resilience. I felt the anxiety that comes with sharing sensitive and controversial material, and it didn't hold me back.

I am a living, breathing example that there is hope for our young women and, with hard work and support of their loved ones, they can thrive. For this reason, *Conscious Empowerment* contains my own challenges with self-esteem and confidence, along with interviews with many other incredible individuals. My passion for helping girls far outweighs my fear of being judged or misunderstood.

The first ever large-scale national survey on confidence, called Girls' Index, was designed to develop a deeper understanding of the thoughts, experiences, perceptions, beliefs, behaviors, and attitudes of teen girls throughout the United States.

Dr. Lisa Hinkelman, founder and CEO of Ruling Our eXperiences (ROX), surveyed girls from fifth through twelfth grade and found:

"The percentage of girls who would describe themselves as confident declines more than 25 percent throughout the middle school years, from 86 percent to 60 percent."[1]

---

1   Lisa Hinkelman, *The Girls' Index: New Insights into the Complex World of Today's Girls* (Columbus: Ruling Our eXperiences, Inc, 2017), 8.

This suggests girls' confidence drastically declines around puberty.

There is also a need to develop more customized approaches for supporting young women from diverse backgrounds. I have always believed when working with any individual, we must take into consideration *cura personalis*, Latin for "care for the entire person." Race, culture, ethnicity, socioeconomic status, gender expression, and sexual orientation play major roles in how we view ourselves. Recently, there has been an increase in visibility of social justice movements surrounding women and people of color.

Dr. Kimberlé Crenshaw—critical race theorist, social justice advocate, and feminist law professor and researcher—developed the term *intersectionality*. The concept highlights how individuals are simultaneously shaped by each of their group memberships and identities. Crenshaw explains intersectionality by saying, "You can't just take the experiences of a Black man and a white woman and put them together to describe a Black woman's experience. A Black woman's experience is not the sum total."[2] Initiating conversations about intersectionality is vital as we shape social justice movements and determine the best ways to empower young women.

In respecting all of the qualities that make a girl unique, we give her permission to be her authentic self. This increases the likelihood of her being able to display confidence in a

---

2   Lelia Gowland, "How Your Racial and Gender Identities Can Overlap and Affect Your Career," *Forbes*, June 27, 2018.

variety of areas in her life. This book will further explore what intersectionality is and why it matters when we help young women.

As an adolescent, my struggle with self-esteem caused me to lack confidence in my abilities and hindered me from being my authentic self. I remember feeling insecure in more than one area of my life growing up. The boys in middle school would poke fun at my hairy arms during gym class, so I always wore long-sleeve shirts. I hated wearing light-colored clothing during elementary school because I was embarrassed about my sweat showing. I only wore dark colors. Maybe this was why I was the only girl in my class who didn't join the soccer or basketball teams.

There were times throughout high school I didn't love the skin I was in. I used a tanning bed so my skin had a brighter glow and my muscles looked more toned. I went back again and again, despite knowing repeated use could cause cancer. I constantly looked at my stomach in the mirror, obsessing over whether or not it was flat enough. When I got lower than an A on my report card, I was disappointed in myself. When I failed, I struggled to move forward. I often got stuck in negative thoughts and couldn't seem to find a way out.

I got caught up in the culture of comparison. In college, I became so engrossed in social media I convinced myself I had to look like the bodybuilding competitors on Instagram. I weighed my food to the ounce for a short period of time. I looked great on the outside, but on the inside, I hated who I was.

Thankfully, I had friends who challenged my thoughts and behaviors and helped me break away from these toxic patterns. Through a lot of internal work and support, I was able to overcome many of the challenges I faced. It is possible anxiety and struggling with self-acceptance will continue to creep up now and again in my life, but I no longer let them control me. I use the skills I've learned through my education, research, and therapy to cope with stressors. I am slowly starting to accept the fact I might always be "high strung," and my imperfections make me who I am: driven, charismatic, and passionate.

I am proud I stepped outside my comfort zone to go on an immersion trip to Nicaragua toward the end of my college career. I had the opportunity to experience an entirely different culture and way of life. This trip was meant to serve as an educational experience. We did not help build or fix; we simply listened and learned. We did a lot of reflecting, helping me remember resources like running water are not guaranteed. Trying to carry pails of water uphill was no easy feat, even for a girl like me who lifts. I remember declining help from my host mother and shortly after needing assistance. Even in the small moments, I was learning humility.

As I was exposed to diverse cultures, I found myself increasingly interested in lives different from my own. During my time at John Carroll University, I began working as a physical education teacher for first to sixth grade girls at an Orthodox Jewish school in Cleveland. When I started this position, I felt uncomfortable, like an outsider. As someone who grew up Catholic, I initially knew little about the Jewish faith. I took steps to educate myself, and over time, I grew a love for the community. I started an after-school program and partnered with the school counselor to run social-skills groups throughout my four years at the school. This experience helped me recognize the importance of carefully tailoring programs with cultural sensitivity.

After a couple years working in the school, I developed the Empowered & Poised movement. Empowered & Poised programs teach young women fundamental skills that enhance social, mental, and physical well-being. This book, as well as the Empowered & Poised movement, provide tools to help girls realize their true beauty from the inside out.

I also learned certain topics that are appropriate for one community are not always appropriate for the next. Empowered & Poised programming is customized to meet the needs of each community we serve.

On my website, I shared with the Empowered & Poised community,

> *Life can be tough as a girl. The constant criticisms we receive can be downright brutal. Nothing ever seems to be good enough in the eyes of society. My desire is to create a movement that helps build girls into Empowered and Poised women by teaching them fundamental skills focused on social, mental, and physical well-being. This movement will allow girls to see they are perfect just the way they are!*

I made it my goal to be a light, empowering individuals from a young age to love themselves because I didn't want them to face challenges in the same way I did.

Empowered & Poised has allowed me to meet young women like fifth-grader Caroline. She was selected as a participant for the fifteen-week girls group. This program is typically run as a lunch bunch group in schools. It consists of journaling, discussion, and hands-on activities that all promote social–emotional development. Caroline was recommended for this program by her school counselor who had noticed she lacked confidence.

When she began the semester, she spoke under her breath and averted her gaze when sharing with the small group. By the end of the program, she was able to speak up loud and proud. On her post-program survey, she shared, "I learned to be confident and believe in myself." Caroline wrote that the only thing she would change about the program was to make it longer!

Because of my positive experiences with Empowered & Poised and my desire to continue to work on myself and better the world, I decided to go back to school to obtain my master's in social work. My social work education and diverse circle of friends further challenged me to look at my own biases and privileged statuses. I am grateful to have had the opportunity to explore deeper how childhood, historical, and racial trauma can shape an individual's experiences and development.

I later took a course called Theories of Oppression, which taught me about intersectionality. I learned how someone can have privilege in one area of life while being oppressed in another. I am white. I am also female. I continue to confront my ongoing implicit biases and explore societal structures' impacts on minority groups. This can be tough. Few people wake up in the morning saying, "I want to be ignorant or unknowingly hurt other people." Just because they don't want this doesn't mean it doesn't happen. There have been times, as I have been learning, when I said dumb stuff and wished I hadn't. However, it takes strength to have hard conversations.

Finally, living with a Black man has opened my eyes to so much knowledge I never thought I needed to know. Out of respect for him, I will not share his personal experiences, but I am thankful he has allowed me into his life and has been vulnerable sharing the unique challenges he continues to face. I will never fully understand all he has overcome. I do know, over the past five years, my desire to learn about the minority experience has deepened. He has taught me a tremendous amount about life. Words cannot express the positive impact he has had on me and my drive to be a good ally.

I have had to admit to "not knowing" more than a few times throughout my journey. This book was one more way for me to learn about others. I am eternally grateful for all the individuals who have opened up their lives and shared their stories. Conversations are key to learning.

I will openly admit: I do not have all of the answers. This book is just a starting point for exploring how a girl's unique background impacts her development of self-esteem and confidence, and how adults can support her in mindful and positive ways.

This book provides examples from numerous backgrounds; however, this book is primarily focused on race, culture, and socioeconomic status. Particular groups that are not further discussed are girls with disabilities (both visible and invisible) and girls within the LGBTQIA+ community.

We live in a society where infrastructure (transportation, school curriculum, buildings, etc.) is often not accessible to all people. As someone who supports girls with disabilities, you must mindfully notice any barriers to access that may send a message to individuals that they do not matter or they do not belong. It is essential that as adults, we empower girls with disabilities to advocate for themselves and support them in identifying strengths in their differences.

Girls who identify within the LGBTQIA+ community are often ostracized and can experience little support from adults and peers in their lives. Transgender girls are subject to the most criticism and scrutiny of perhaps any subgroup of girls. Girls who identify as LGBTQIA+ deserve to be honored and brought into conversations surrounding development of self-esteem and confidence. It is essential all girls and adults feel included within this discussion.

It is my belief that even though the interviews conducted did not have a primary focus on girls with disabilities or girls who identify as LGBTQIA+, the information provided can be used as a tool to tailor an approach that works for you as an adult who supports girls.

I've realized girls aren't the only ones who need support; caregivers and educators need support too! After over ten years of working with young women and countless hours of research, I learned the importance of equipping adults with tools for guiding girls through the most turbulent times in their lives. Much of the current information available fails to consider the role of intersectionality in girls' self-image.

In addition to doing extensive research for this book, I had the opportunity to interview a diverse group of over thirty individuals, including psychologists, social workers, doctors, educators, researchers, founders of female empowerment organizations, and young women.

When I asked interviewees for this book the question "How do race, culture, ethnic background, and socioeconomic status impact the development of a girl's confidence?" the most common answer was "I think a better question is how do they not? They impact every aspect of a girl's confidence." Conversely, I received the response, "They don't. It never happened with me, so…" This response is precisely the reason why this book is so vital. Adults who live and work with girls must consider what makes each individual girl unique, even if they have trouble relating to her experience.

This book will explore the intricacies of growing up female, as well as how we can support girls of all backgrounds as they develop. Confidence *can* be taught, just like other skills.

Conscious empowerment is the idea a girl's background should be taken into consideration when we're assisting her in the development of self-esteem and confidence. It is being aware and mindful of what we say to her, where she comes from, and the experiences she has had. We must look at the whole person when determining how to best "empowHER."

I will discuss this idea in greater detail, and I will utilize examples throughout the book to paint a more vivid picture of how we can utilize conscious empowerment to support young women.

Movements for equity, inclusion, and social justice have gained new energy in the past year, and the conversations must continue. Conscious empowerment isn't just an attitude; it is a commitment to building a skill set that takes education, humility, and focus. And it's the informed approach the girls we work with need to feel truly seen and valued. If you're a parent, mentor, coach, teacher, or ally for young women, the time to get on board with conscious empowerment is now.

All of the stories in this book are real stories, lived by real people. Names with an asterisk have been changed for confidentiality purposes.

The chapters are broken up into hashtags (#), because each chapter represents a topic that was "trending" in the thirty-five interviews conducted. In other words, each # represents a main theme that came up time and time again. While there is a plethora of ways to help girls outside of these trending topics, the experts on self-esteem and confidence honed in on these as the most efficient and effective ways to help girls from virtually any background.

CHAPTER 1

INTERSECTIONALITY

In a world where so many people want to fit in, we need to empower girls to embrace their individuality while appreciating the uniqueness of others. Maya Angelou stated, "It is time for parents to teach young people early on that in diversity there is beauty and there is strength."

Before we dive deeper into conscious empowerment and its role in supporting girls' development of self-esteem and confidence, we must first explore the terms *intersectional lens* and *intersectional feminism*.

UN Women, an organization focused on gender equality and the empowerment of women, states, "Using an intersectional lens…means recognizing the historical contexts surrounding an issue. Long histories of violence and systematic discrimination have created deep inequities that disadvantage some from the outset. These inequalities intersect with each other, for example, poverty, caste systems, racism and sexism, denying people their rights and equal opportunities."[3]

---

3   Women, UN, "Intersectional Feminism: What It Means and Why It Matters Right Now," Medium, July 1, 2020.

Historically, feminist movements have been dominated by the voices of middle- and upper-class, heterosexual, white women. They failed to take into account intersectionality. Empowering girls is typically approached with a similarly narrow lens. Kimberlé Crenshaw coined the term *intersectional feminism* to define a distinct feminism that is inclusive of all women's voices and experiences, not just those of the privileged. Crenshaw's definition of intersectionality was based on a theoretical framework developed by Black feminist scholar-activists in the 1970s. The intersectional feminist framework has helped expand the definition of feminism and its scope.

Intersectional feminism is the idea that while fighting for equality for women, we must take into account certain important realities. "Those who are most impacted by gender-based violence, and by gender inequalities, are also the most impoverished and marginalized—Black and brown women, Indigenous women, women in rural areas, young girls, girls living with disabilities, trans youth, and gender nonconforming youth,"[4] explains Majandra Rodriguez Acha, a youth leader and climate justice advocate from Lima, Peru.

To be clear, feminism, as discussed in this book, is about individuals of all genders achieving equitable rights and opportunities. Equitable means fair and reasonable. When working with girls, there may be times where one individual requires extra love and affection during a given moment. Each individual may need different amounts of guidance and support throughout her unique journey to confidence.

---

4   Ibid.

Therefore, feminism is not about one gender being better, stronger, or more capable than others; it is about equality of genders in all arenas of life. We must not discount biological differences, but rather break down the barriers that have been built as a result of years of oppression and socialization.

These walls have caused women and girls to doubt themselves, their abilities, and their worth.

Sadly, it's no surprise "seven in ten girls believe that they are not good enough or don't measure up in some way, including their looks, performance in school, and relationships with friends and family members."[5]

Marissa Buendicho grew up as a girl of Filipino/Pacific Islander (Native Chamorro) descent in Hawaii, and she bravely shared her own story about how her background influenced her self-esteem and confidence growing up. In her culture, people struggled with a widely internalized understanding that being "more white" was desirable. She was taught her language was "less than." Tears filled her eyes as she shared how her ancestors weren't allowed to talk to each other in their native tongue and how slave owners would physically separate families. Her ancestors used broken English as a

---

5   StrategyOne and Ann Kearney-Cooke, *Real Girls, Real Pressure: A National Report on the State of Self-Esteem* (New York City, NY: American Association of University Women, 2008), 1.

way to revolt. Sadly, years later, language continues to be a reminder of the challenges her ancestors faced.

She shared that a handful of her family members went to language schools to learn how to speak better English. She was saddened by the fact that because she was not allowed to speak Filipino growing up, she fully lost her ability to do so. She was also prohibited from speaking Pidgin outside of the home, but was expected to speak it in the home. "If you speak too white inside the home, you look like you're trying to show off to your other family members who didn't get enough education. So, you grow up feeling very confused," she said. Growing up, she would be grounded when speaking her native language, Pidgin. Hawaiian Creole English is also known in Hawaii as Pidgin; this language is an amalgamation of Japanese, Chinese, Filipino, Hawaiian, and Portuguese. Her friends shared similar stories, stating, "I got grounded for speaking 'too white' or 'not white enough.'"

Furthermore, she shared that her friends would often get skin-whitening soap and lotion for the holidays. Families often thought having fairer skin would help their children get into college. Growing up, despite her friends going through similar experiences, they never talked about these issues or reflected deeper because they were both normalized and very painful. Themes in Marissa's story can be found in the stories of many young women currently growing up in the United States. Whether we recognize it or not, pressures to assimilate to a "white ideal" abound in our culture, even today.

Marissa has grown into a talented and accomplished woman and practices as a licensed social worker. The aforementioned comments, actions, and traumas she has faced have been rooted deep inside her and still greatly impact her today. She has chosen to take everything she has learned from her own experiences and education and now works as a psychotherapist and advocate. She truly understands the importance of empowering young women through the lens of intersectional feminism and, more specifically, through utilizing conscious empowerment.

Dr. Tyffani Dent—licensed psychologist; cofounder of Centering Sisters, LLC, an organization dedicated to projects that center the needs of Black women, girls, and femmes; and author of multiple books written to support young women—expanded on Dr. Kimberlé Crenshaw's concept of intersectionality in a way that emphasizes why there is a need for conscious empowerment. She stated, "When you're looking at racial justice issues, those movements value race. When you bring in how that looks based on gender, we don't want to have that conversation. Feminist spaces don't want to deal with race, and so there's nowhere for you to go. When it's time for someone to fight for you, who's fighting for you? Because movement spaces only want to fight for a part of you and tell you the other pieces don't matter."

We must start to consciously empower girls to take the concept of intersectionality one step further. Embolden young women to feel confident in authentically expressing themselves in their entirety: race, culture, ethnicity, gender, and all of the other characteristics and experiences that make them unique. Help them be brave and have tough conversations about the issues they're facing, despite society telling them to sit down and be quiet. Perhaps if society had embraced this idea of conscious empowerment during the time Marissa was growing up, life wouldn't have been as challenging for her.

CHAPTER 2

BUILDING CONFIDENCE

———

I can. I will. I am worthy.

These are all things a self-assured woman says.

But how can we help young women move away from phrases like "I can't" and "I'm not"?

Prior to discovering how to help a young woman build her self-esteem and confidence, we first must understand the difference between these two terms. We often hear these words used interchangeably. While they are similar in nature, they are not the same. *Psychology Today* has simply defined the terms for us:

- "Self-esteem: 'Esteem' is derived from the Latin *aestimare*, meaning 'to appraise, value, rate, weigh, estimate,' and self-esteem is our cognitive and, above all, emotional appraisal of our own worth. More than that, it is the matrix through which we think, feel, and act, and reflects and determines our relation to ourselves, to others, and to the world.

- Self-confidence: 'Confidence' comes from the Latin *fidere*, 'to trust.' To be self-confident is to trust in oneself, and, in particular, in one's ability or aptitude to engage successfully or at least adequately with the world. A self-confident person is ready to rise to new challenges, seize opportunities, deal with difficult situations, and take responsibility if and when things go awry."[6]

National expert in health and wellness Dr. Fernstrom wrote an article called "Self-esteem vs. self-confidence—and how to boost both!" In it, she explains self-esteem is "inward facing" and self-confidence is "outward facing." Her article shared some great examples that help us better understand each term. Self-esteem can be displayed in the following ways: avoiding negative self-talk, being able to say yes or no when you choose, resilience, good grooming and lifestyle habits, and appreciating the skills of others. Meanwhile, self-confidence may be manifested as asking for help when needed, avoiding judging other people, not being afraid to be wrong, appreciating and trusting our own abilities, being flexible and adaptable, and delivering on commitments.[7]

It is possible to be highly confident in one area and insecure in another. For example, I am confident in my ability to connect with others, but I lack confidence when it comes to mathematics. Confidence can be fluid. I saw this when teaching physical education to elementary-aged children. I

---

6   Neel Burton, "Self-Confidence versus Self-Esteem," *Psychology Today.* Sussex Publishers, October 19, 2015.

7   Madelyn Fernstrom, "Dr. Fernstrom: Self-Esteem vs. Self-Confidence—and How to Boost Both!" *NBCNews.com.* NBCUniversal News Group, May 24, 2019.

developed a gymnastics unit, which was the very first time many students were exposed to this sport. In the beginning, many of the girls were terrified to try some of the most basic skills like a somersault. They were afraid of embarrassing themselves or getting hurt; however, by the end of the unit, girls were eager to try cartwheels and backbends. Because of encouragement and practice, nearly all of the students were confident in their ability to successfully complete the basic skills taught in class.

Unfortunately, confidence as a whole declines drastically over time. *Real Girls, Real Pressure: A National Report on the State of Self-Esteem* shared that more than half of girls (one out of two, or 56 percent) claimed to experience a drop in confidence at puberty.[8] Typically, puberty happens during adolescence, which follows middle childhood. Children are roughly six to eleven years old during middle childhood and twelve to eighteen years old during adolescence. During middle childhood, it is typical to see increased independence from family, friendships growing in importance, and increased peer pressure. Meanwhile, during adolescence, an individual may notice physical maturation, increased concern about looks, intensified moods, less affection towards parents, and increased capacity for more intimate relationships. These are the two basic periods or stages of development this book will be focused on.

The Girls' Index *Girls, Diversity & the Future Impact* report states, "Overall, 26 percent fewer girls describe themselves as

---

8   Stephanie Herzfeld, "New Social Experiment by Always® Reveals Harmful Impact Commonly Used Phrase Has on Girls," *Procter & Gamble*, updated December 2, 2020.

confident in high school as compared to elementary school. Girls who identify as multiracial experience the most significant decline throughout their school years (-24 percent), and Black girls experience the smallest decline (-12 percent) in their confidence levels."[9]

Juliann Garey's article "Raising Girls With Healthy Self-Esteem" highlighted a key point: "'As girls physically mature,' says Douglas Bunnell, PhD, 'they actually develop more body fat and that's really sort of a trigger for menstruation. So, in that sense, the things that are attached to growth and development for girls are really negatively valued by society.'"[10] Therefore, as unfortunate as it is, it is not uncommon for girls to be uncomfortable in their own bodies for a period of time.

I vividly remember my own confidence and self-esteem dropping somewhere between middle childhood and adolescence. It was awkward going through many changes that happen as you mature—growing hair in new places, becoming curvier, and managing the intense emotions that sometimes surround menstruation. I remember my mom handing me the American Girl book *The Care & Keeping of You* so I could understand the "weird" and "scary" things my body was going through, yet these are very normal processes.

I learned more about this when I spoke to *Sue, the mother of a freshman in high school, and she noted she's seen her

---

9   Lisa Hinkelman & Sibyl West, *Girls, Diversity & the Future: A Girls' Index Impact Report*. The Girls' Index (Columbus: Ruling Our eXperiences, Inc., 2020), 4.

10   Juliann Garey, "Raising Girls with Healthy Self-Esteem," *Child Mind Institute*, July 28, 2020.

daughter's confidence ebb and flow over time. Her daughter shared with her her most unconfident time was in fifth or sixth grade. Sue also shared that her daughter often says things like "you don't understand." The truth is, sometimes as adults, we feel far removed from our younger years, and with a shift in culture, we may actually not understand. For this reason, Sue shared the importance of not diminishing a girl's feelings. While something might not seem like a big deal to us, it is still important to validate a young woman's feelings and where she is currently in her life.

According to Jillian Lampert, PhD, MPH, RD, LD, FAED, and chief strategy officer at The Emily Program (an eating disorder treatment center), it is not abnormal for there to be a push and pull during middle childhood and adolescence. She shared a great example from a fifth-grader, *Crystal, to demonstrate how this plays out in real life. Crystal's family did not have the resources to buy brand-name clothing, which often becomes more important to many girls during this stage of development. However, at home, her family was very big on body confidence and self-love, and did not place much value on brand names. So, she felt stuck between the messages at home and from her peers at school. Dr. Lampert could see the "wrestling match" happening during this time when peer influence begins to grow. This greatly challenged Crystal, similar to many other girls who are in this stage of development where they feel they're being "pulled between two worlds"—family and peers. It was not so much that she cared about not being able to get the clothing as it was the fact she wanted to have the continued support of her family while fitting in with her peers. Thus, it was difficult for

Crystal to know how to properly proceed to keep both relationships strong.

Both nature (genetics/hormones) and nurture (environment) also play a role in the development of a young woman. The changes young women go through as they grow and mature will inevitably be different than the changes boys go through. However, when it comes to environment, adults play a large role in the way we socialize children, which impacts how they grow and develop.

Dr. Naama Barnea-Goraly, child and adolescent psychiatrist and founder of Girltelligence, an app for girls, shared in her interview for this book that we treat boys and girls differently, starting from birth. This can perpetuate gender roles. She believes it is important to celebrate our differences while modeling equality. For example, we can buy girls toys like building blocks, teach them how to use tools, and model that household chores can be split evenly between men and women. This can help girls realize from a young age they are just as capable as men.

When working with and empowering girls from backgrounds that differ from our own, we must be both culturally sensitive and culturally humble. In other words, we should never assume to know everything about the background of the individual with whom we are working but, rather, allow space for her to share about her experiences in her own time. Race, culture, ethnicity, and socioeconomic status, among other variables, can largely contribute to a young woman's development.

Additionally, we must be mindful of various traditions as they relate to growth, development, and womanhood. Lindsey Compton, executive director at White Buffalo Calf Women's Society, highlights the importance of celebrating a young woman's coming-of-age, especially in the Indigenous community. In the Indigenous community, the Isnati coming-of-age ceremony can last up to four days and four nights, which happens after a woman begins her first menstruation. During this time, she is taught and celebrated by other women in her tribe. This is a sacred ceremony that promotes tribal unity and self-identity, reminds young women of the power of intergenerational support, and provides familial healing.

Similar traditions can be found in other cultures, such as sweet sixteen celebrations, bat mitzvahs, and quinceañeras. Some families and cultures place more importance on these coming-of-age rituals than others, so it's most crucial to be mindful of the traditions within and outside of your community. Ultimately, to consciously empower girls, we need to take into consideration all variables that play a role in their development of self-esteem and confidence.

CHAPTER 3

#BETHATADULT

Be the person who champions the girls in your life: your daughters, students, athletes, and mentees. Create space for them. We all know how easy it is to want to multitask and respond while in the middle of a million other things, myself included. Stop what you are doing and turn your undivided attention to the young woman. Truly listen. Make it a priority to cancel out the noise in your life and be fully present.

It is important girls feel heard. For parents, this might look like stepping away from your work for a few moments when your daughter needs a loving embrace or to vent about her tough day at school. For educators, this might mean inviting a group of students to your room during lunch period to work through a challenge that has come up inside or outside the classroom. For a coach, this may require pulling a player aside to give her some positive reinforcement after getting discouraged because of missing a few goals or shots. For a mentor, this might mean reaching out and setting up a time to go for a walk to catch up about how your mentee's week was, even if they don't initiate the conversation on their own. In other words, being that adult means being authentic and genuinely caring and creating space to validate a girl and her feelings not when we want to, but when she needs us.

"After decades of forming hypotheses, conducting surveys, crafting and rewriting definitions, analyzing data, and writing journal articles, Search Institute researchers and practitioners have arrived at a surprisingly simple conclusion: Nothing—nothing—has more impact in the life of a child than positive relationships."[11] The Search Institute identified five elements that make relationships powerful in young people's lives. These elements comprise the Relationships First Developmental Framework and state that young people who experience strong developmental relationships are far more likely to report social–emotional strength. Thus, helping a young person develop a clearer sense of self leads to higher levels of self-esteem and confidence.

"Meaningful relationships are characterized by a dynamic give and take that shapes who we are as we grow, change, and encounter new challenges and circumstances."[12] It's important to both "be that adult" as well as help diversify the number and types of positive adult role models the girls we work and live with have in their lives.

Interestingly, "it is often assumed that socioeconomic status is predictive of resources and, therefore, support. However, The Girls' Index data indicates that more girls who attend high-poverty schools report having supportive adults in their

---

11   Eugene Roehlkepartain et al., *New Research Report* (Minneapolis, MN: Search Institute, 2018), 3.

12   Ibid.

lives as compared to girls who attend schools with the lowest amounts of poverty (79.8 percent versus 70.4 percent)."[13]

My first summer after graduating college, I had the opportunity to run a summer camp for a group of girls in a vulnerable population. Of the dozens of camps and workshops I've run, this session and the girls in it hold a special place in my heart. We never like to admit it, but when working with youths, there are always a few students who stand out among their peers. There was one young lady in seventh grade who I will never forget: *Dee. Dee was thin, well-endowed, and wore shoes with holes in them, causing her toes to poke out. She was feisty, yet I knew about girls like her—girls who try to hide their fears and insecurities by breaking the rules and testing boundaries. She was hiding from herself and the pain she was dealing with inside. She ached for attention from an adult, which was shown by her acting out.

Dee's counselor warned me she was "trouble," so I made it a goal to connect with her on a one-on-one basis. At the end of the day, I would offer to stay longer, in case anyone wanted to discuss anything private. Dee took advantage of this opportunity nearly every chance she got. During these moments, she opened up and shared about the struggles she had at home, with boys, and in her personal life.

Dee later told me many of the stories she shared with me were embellished. She did this as a way to "test" me and see if I actually cared about her. I showed her I was there for her by

---

13   Hinkelman, *The Girls' Index: New Insights into the Complex World of Today's Girls*, 8.

balancing being a friend-like figure and an authority figure. I've noticed that with the right balance and boundaries, we can win over most adolescents and establish both mutual trust and respect. Once we establish a safe relationship, it is a lot easier to impact them, ultimately helping them realize their potential.

So, let's consider what this looked like for me and Dee. When I first met her, she was wrapped up in her phone and telling her primary counselor 'no' when given directions on a nearly daily basis. Over time, I was able to guide her toward being kinder to her counselor. We discussed the importance of treating others how she would want to be treated and showing the same level of respect to her other counselor that she did to me. Eventually, she began hiding less behind her phone, which often got her in trouble since phones weren't permitted during camp.

She was proud of herself. She smiled from ear to ear when I acknowledged her progress in this area. She started to realize she was capable of staying off her phone, even though at the beginning of the program, she shared it felt impossible to put her phone down. By the end of just six short weeks, she was able to put her phone away during our sessions of her own volition.

Dee also developed the courage to sing in front of an entire audience of campers and their families for the end of summer finale. She confidently sung the lyrics to the popular song "Scars To Your Beautiful" by Alessia Cara. The song was picked by her and her fellow campers as a way to show their true colors. It reflected something deep. Dee was beautiful just the way she was, even if that was not how she always felt inside. She realized she was capable of self-composure, singing in front of a crowd, and being herself.

At the end of every camp, students shared what they learned. Dee chose to share a goal she set for herself. Her goal stated, "I would like to try to [continue to] keep myself off the phone most of the time." This is a testament to how positive organizations and mentorship can help a girl to become more confident in herself and her abilities. Dee also stated, "I learned I don't have to be another person. I can be myself." She was able be herself without hiding behind a screen or disruptive behavior.

It's important to note self-expression is different for everyone. Thankfully, Dr. Dent, licensed psychologist and expert on issues impacting Black girls, understood this and was there to support students throughout her career.

Dr. Dent emphasized the need to recognize girlhood and the various expressions of it. It isn't about how we feel girls should be, but about supporting them as they are. Dr. Dent shared powerful stories about her advocacy on behalf of girls in the classroom.

One young lady she remembered well was *Tasha. Tasha was a Black student constantly talked about in the break room among teachers because she was viewed as loud and disrespectful. Dr. Dent took it upon herself to check out the situation by sitting in the classroom. After observing, she realized Tasha was not being disrespectful; she was attempting to advocate for herself. So, Dr. Dent helped both Tasha and the teacher reframe the situation. Dr. Dent articulated, "What I am hearing is Tasha standing up for herself. What I am hearing is that when Tasha views something as a problem, she has the bravery to be able to acknowledge that something needs to change." Dr. Dent would say to Tasha, "Wow! That's amazing that you're able to do that!" We should encourage girls from all backgrounds to speak up and out. We must also be mindful not to allow our own biases to get in the way of hearing what a girl is saying. In other words, we need to treat all girls with the same respect and expectation that they can and should voice their opinions.

Dr. Dent's encouragement helped Tasha sit a bit taller. We have the ability to help other girls like Tasha do the same. Tasha began to realize these traits she possessed were admirable. However, it was clear no one ever told her these qualities were good but, rather, reasons to be denigrated and punished. This can often be seen when girls are told they are "too loud" and "too bossy" when they're really speaking up and being assertive.

Dr. Dent shared we must "acknowledge that as a society…we view what is acceptable and wanted is from a framework of closer to whiteness. Anything that goes further away from that on the continuum is less desirable." Therefore, "Everybody needs to look at how we have internalized and passed messages on to the next generation, because we have our own self-esteem issues that we need to address," shared Dr. Dent.

It can be difficult to be the models young women need us to be. It is often easier to talk about our shortcomings than our strengths. However, **to be the adult girls need, we have to**

focus on our own growth journey, all while helping them on theirs. Sometimes helping girls on their journey means assisting them with daily struggles they face, like doing their hair.

Dr. Dent shared that for Black girls in particular, emphasis on hair often comes from a place of internalized oppression. Internalized oppression is when a marginalized group uses the methods of the oppressor against itself. Historically, Black hair texture has been viewed as unpresentable in its natural form.

Unfortunately, not all girls have the means to go to a fancy boutique hair salon to get their hair dolled up. This was the reality for *Olivia. Olivia often wore a scarf over her hair because she didn't have the time or finances to buy the proper products to keep up with the ideals society set for her. Olivia often got teased by her classmates for not having her hair done. Even worse, she would get in trouble at school for wearing a scarf to cover it up and refusing to take it off.

When the school tried to suspend Olivia for wearing her hair scarf, she became increasingly irritated. Dr. Dent recognized this and took it upon herself to advocate for Olivia, just as she had with Tasha. She invited Olivia to her office and had her take off her scarf. She helped Olivia to put her hair into a ponytail. Unfortunately, this did not take away the negative comments about the way she looked. Sadly, because of this, Olivia struggled to see her own beauty.

Olivia is not unique in feeling pressure to look a certain way. In fact, "98 percent of girls feel there is an immense pressure from external sources to look a certain way."[14] This percentage is overwhelming and devastating. We must remind girls of what is most important, and that's what is on the inside. Additionally, we must take time to learn about what is important to each individual regarding her appearance, helping her take pride in who she is as an individual. Oftentimes, the clothes we wear, the way we do our hair, and how we present ourselves are ways of representing where we come from and how we feel about ourselves. We must empower girls to stand tall so beauty can radiate out from within.

American actress and singer Amandla Stenberg shared with *Teen Vogue* that she's sick of talking about her hair. She stated, "I'm not tired of talking about hair in the sense of it being an empowering thing. I know when I used to chemically straighten mine, I did it because I wasn't comfortable with my natural hair. I thought it was too poofy, too kinky. So, for me, personally, when I started wearing it natural, it felt like I was blossoming because I was letting go of all the dead hair and all the parts of me that had rejected my natural state. But, you know, it's not like that for all Black girls. Some have their hair straight because that's just how they like it, and it doesn't mean that they accept themselves any less."

Help girls to embrace themselves however they wish and are comfortable. Don't make assumptions about girls without getting to know and understand them as individuals.

---

14 StrategyOne and Ann Kearney-Cooke, *Real Girls, Real Pressure: A National Report on the State of Self-Esteem* (New York City, NY: American Association of University Women, 2008), 1.

Some girls like their hair straight; some like it crimped or curly. Some wear it natural, and others prefer it styled. All are beautiful, and as adults, we should be mindful of letting them know that however they wish to express themselves and their girlhood is perfectly acceptable.

Society places too much emphasis on superficial things. We also need to help girls realize they are more than their looks.

> We shouldn't just be telling girls they are pretty. We should be telling them they are smart. They are kind. They are capable.

Dr. Alexander, a school psychologist with a PhD in urban education, made it a priority to embrace students from all backgrounds. She vividly remembers working with *Ebony, who transferred into a predominantly white, affluent school culture. At first, Ebony did not feel like she fit in. She was one of few African American girls in her school. As if trying to figure out who you are is not already hard enough for girls at this age, now it was apparent to her she was different. Not only could Ebony feel it deep within, she could see it in the mirror too. For this reason, she constantly questioned herself. She questioned things such as her clothing and food choices, as well as her appearance. She became so insecure that any time she would get reprimanded by her teachers, she believed it was because of her race. "People must be treating me like this because they don't like me," she would say. While her feelings were real, this was far from the truth, especially when it came to Dr. Alexander.

Dr. Alexander made it a priority to work with this young lady and help set her up for success. She enrolled her in lunch groups with a diverse set of peers who extended kindness and compassion towards her. These girls helped her to feel welcome. They helped her to navigate the bell schedule, which was different from her previous school. Prior to having these young ladies as a support system, Ebony was rather overwhelmed by switching classes every period; but because of their encouragement, she became confident in her ability to transition throughout the day. Over time, with the help and support of her peers and Dr. Alexander, she blossomed. She began to realize when a teacher asked her to sit down, it was not because of her race or because she was disliked; she was asked to sit down simply because it was a class rule.

She gained the confidence to take risks, ask questions, and try new things. She started playing the flute, which she grew to love. She discovered her voice and gained the ability to speak up and advocate for herself even when it felt scary.

Dr. Alexander made sure to listen to Ebony and assist her in exploring her interests. Most importantly, she realized Ebony was unique and talented in her own way. She treated her with individualized care. Dr. Alexander made it a goal to ensure Ebony found success within her current skill set so she could develop the confidence it took to be the Poised girl she always was.

Do not miss the opportunity to be the Dr. Alexander or Dr. Dent: #BeThatAdult for the girls in your life.

CHAPTER 4

HOW TO: BE
THAT ADULT

———

Dr. Ellen Rome, head of the Cleveland Clinic Children's Center for Adolescent Medicine and professor of pediatrics at the Cleveland Clinic Lerner College of Medicine, shared the importance of being a "lighthouse, instead of a helicopter or snowplow," originally attributed to Ken Ginsberg, author of *Raising Kids to Thrive*. Being a lighthouse means you provide girls with "safe harbor and guidance anytime it's an issue of ethics or safety, yet otherwise help them sail freely on those uncharted waters." It can be extremely difficult to just stand back and not take control of a situation; however, Dr. Rome reminds us, **"Sometimes the best thing we can do to help our [girls learn] and thrive is to get out of their way."** She equates this experience to the parent who helps a toddler get back up after falling. It helps girls build resilience.

HuffPost stated, "Hovering may have backfired. College counselors across the nation are reporting higher rates of general anxiety in this generation's crop of students. And kids who say they had overcontrolling parents have higher levels of depression and reported feeling less satisfied with family life. When they receive parental support they didn't ask for, they feel less competent and have less initiative than peers who weren't parented in this way and lack a sense of confidence because of it."[15] Interestingly, Lee Paiva, founder of No Means No Kenya and IMpower United, recognized through her work girls who are raised in families with over-protective parents are ending up in similar positions to girls who grow up with neglectful parents. She sees them entering unhealthy relationships, withdrawing, developing mental health issues, and turning to unhealthy coping strategies. Thus, she predicts confidence declines due to the fact they have not "learned how to fall and gracefully rise."

One great example of a mother who understands what it means to help her daughter build resilience is Liz Ferro, founder of Girls with Sole and author of *Finish Line Feeling* and *Girls with Sole: A Girl Power Guide to Unleashing Your Inner Superhero*. Liz shared a story about her daughter's eighth grade experience at sleepaway swim camp. Her daughter called complaining about the dorms, which weren't exactly glamorous, but they were safe and temporary. For this reason, Liz let her daughter ride out the experience for the night, unlike her roommate's mother, who came to her rescue. This mother drove from out of state to pick up her daughter and put her in a comfortable hotel room. Unfortunately, when life is too easy, girls don't always have the opportunity to build resiliency and grit.

---

15   Anna Almendrala, "5 Signs You Were Raised by Helicopter Parents," *HuffPost* (blog), updated March 14, 2021.

While it is nearly impossible to get it right every time, being the adult girls need is similar to Goldie Locks: not too hot and hovering, not too cold (literally or metaphorically), but just right. Just right meaning supportive and attentive, while still giving space and room for the girls we work or live with to learn and grow.

Being the adult a girl needs also involves creating space for her. You can invite a student to stop by during lunch or after school to speak with them about their joys and challenges. You can make time to listen to the highs and lows of your child's day during dinner. Sometimes, young people are afraid or uncertain of how to approach adults for help. Knowing this, you can be the one to reach out first to show young people you are there for them and genuinely care.

While it can be difficult to do, it is also important to be consistent in your efforts to connect and also follow through with your promises. Retired educator Andrea Pollock shared that in the many years of working with youth, one of the greatest lessons she can share with others is the importance of consistency. "[You must] be there and do what you say you're going to do, because that's what everyone's looking for—a sense of belonging and feeling like somebody really believes in you."

Stephanie Hull, president and CEO of Girls Inc., warns you must be willing and prepared to hear anything during conversations where you allow a safe place for girls to open up. Some things you hear may be unsettling. You may also be at a loss for words, in which case Stephanie suggests you can share, "I've not ever thought about this before, and I don't really know what to say, but I'm glad that we are talking. Let's keep talking." Further, she advises, "[We must] create space in [our] own mind for truly just being there and not necessarily solving [our children's problems] ...maybe shoulder the burden of not being able to handle something that the girl can't handle." You can have girls write out a list of pros and cons in order to problem solve and make their own decisions.

When I work with girls through Empowered & Poised, I always like to offer them an opportunity to speak with me privately after session or submit a question in the "question/ treasure box." The box is a place where girls can submit questions anonymously and have them answered without the fear of judgement. Rather than getting false information online or from friends, they can ask a trusted adult. I tend to answer the questions the following week for two reasons. First, it is important students can sneak their questions in the box at the last minute when no one else is looking. And secondly, this additional time allows me to consult other professionals regarding questions that are extremely sensitive, as well as come up with a thoughtful response. Giving girls the option to use the box, speak one-on-one, and have their stories heard allows them to feel a sense of control, thus giving root to empowerment.

Showing girls we don't know everything is a great way to demonstrate they don't have to be perfect. It is also critical to model self-acceptance and self-love, and especially to be mindful not to shame ourselves in front of them. Girls take note of your actions. They see when we talk about things like our thick thighs, lack of knowledge, or others in a negative way.

Don't just tell them how to be confident: Show them.

This may also mean normalizing working on yourself in a healthy manner through exercise, therapy, or journaling. When we show girls how we positively persevere through challenges, we are teaching them they can too!

KEY TAKEAWAYS

- Teach them skills and guide them to building resilience.
- Consistently create space to listen to them.
- Be a good model.
- Some girls might prefer us to laugh with them when they are struggling while others may need a shoulder to cry on. Both scenarios are okay and normal! Be present for them.

Reflection: Reflect on and write three to five ways I have been a good role model for the girl(s) in my life. What two barriers prevent me from being less than my best for her/them? What's one actionable step I can take this week to begin to eliminate these barriers?

_____

_____

_____

_____

_____

_____

_____

_____

_____

_____

_____

_____

CHAPTER 5

#EXPOSURE

———

"Look at your young person's comfort zone...[and determine] how to give them the opportunity to go further and show themselves that they can," shared Simone Marean, CEO of Girls Leadership. Girls need opportunities to learn about new people, places, and things they haven't yet had the chance to explore. A girl may be a naturally gifted actress or poet, but if she is not exposed to seeing a play, hearing spoken word, or other forms of expression, that talent may remain unearthed. It is beneficial to expose girls to a wide variety of experiences in all areas: academics, arts, sciences, sports, people, etc.

Dr. Damary Bonilla-Rodriguez, EdD, a national authority on leadership development (especially as it pertains to diversity and inclusion), shared her thoughts regarding growing up as a Latinx girl in America. Being a woman of color, she is well aware minorities need to work harder to achieve. Many of the girls she has worked with are both racial minorities and socioeconomically disadvantaged. Sadly, this can lead to a lack of exposure or access in a variety of areas, including resources, opportunities, and experiences. Ultimately, when girls have access to a diverse range of opportunities, mentors, and external events, their worldview is more likely to expand. As a result, they gain confidence in their ability to be successful in life. Dr. Bonilla-Rodriguez says exposure is not only helpful in a girl's development of self-esteem and confidence: It is critical.

She shared a particularly memorable experience in her thirteen years working full-time with the national office of a female empowerment organization, where she was leading the organization's Latina and diversity, equity, and inclusion efforts. She reminisced about her time working with a young woman named *Valentina, whose confidence significantly increased over time. Valentina grew up in Florida in a single-parent home. Her father was an alcoholic and failed to #BeThatAdult for his daughter. Due to her mother's financial struggles, she often signed her up for a variety of free and low-cost programs as a way to help expose her daughter to opportunities she otherwise could not afford. Valentina's ability to join programming expanded her horizons, helping her to see more possibilities for her future.

One organization Valentina's mom signed her up for was Girls Inc., an organization that "equips girls to lead fulfilling and productive lives, break the cycle of poverty, and become role models in their community."[16] She was thrilled to be chosen through this program to travel to New York. Many of the individuals Dr. Bonilla-Rodriguez shared about had never been on a plane, and some had never even traveled outside of their own community due to a lack of financial resources.

---

16   "Home Page," Girls Inc., accessed March 20, 2021.

Valentina ended up becoming a scholar with the organization, which allowed her to continue to travel and explore the United States. Because of these experiences and exposure to new places, Valentina had the courage to move away for college. To her surprise, she was admitted to an Ivy League school: Princeton. Eventually, after graduating, she moved from her small community in Florida all the way out to California. She is now visible online and shares her journey with other girls to inspire them in the same way she was inspired—through educational programming.

Another example in which Dr. Bonilla-Rodriguez highlighted the importance of exposure was in relation to her beloved niece. *Edith grew up facing a plethora of challenges dealing with physical issues. She's had over a dozen surgeries throughout her life. Despite the struggles she faced, she was always resilient and successful in school. However, she never seemed to feel good enough, despite being a warrior. She always felt the need to do more and be more in order to measure up to her peers.

While Edith's life is not always easy, she is fortunate to have a wonderful mother who serves as a strong role model for her. Her mom is a police officer in New York. Edith illustrated a cartoon on her Instagram about heroes, saying she lives with her real-life hero: her mom. Because of her mom, she has been exposed to the field of criminal justice, which she now aspires to enter in her future. Edith was selected as one of the few individuals to spend the summer at the FBI Academy. This allowed her to continue to pursue her passion for the field while further building her knowledge. Edith also looks up to her aunt, Dr. Bonilla-Rodriguez, who is among the 4 percent of Latinx women to have a doctoral degree. Exposure to successful women with whom she can relate, as well as opportunities like the FBI Academy, have helped Edith develop confidence. Despite opportunities and exposure, Dr. Bonilla-Rodriguez notes, Edith still struggles with issues related to self-confidence on a regular basis.

One experience that significantly impacted her niece was when she became homecoming queen as a Latinx girl in a primarily white community. Edith said, "Can you believe I won? There aren't many Hispanic girls in the school." She was shocked! In addition to being a racial minority, she also has visible physical side effects and scars from her disability that cause her to stand out. Winning homecoming queen gave her a bit of hope and helped her to relax from the constant need she felt to prove herself. She realized there are people who accept her just the way she is.

While Edith still struggles with loving herself, she is far better off because of the exposure she's had in her life. Dr. Bonilla-Rodriguez questions what could happen to girls who aren't as lucky as her niece and end up falling through the cracks.

Clarissa Russell, MPH, cofounder of Cleveland's Girls Health Summit, also shared about the importance of exposure for young women. She knows a lack of exposure can lead to girls' growth being hindered: "The influences of the environments in which our young people are being exposed to daily affects self-esteem. What we see around us impacts how a young lady feels about herself and possibly what she may be able to achieve or experience."

Clarissa had the opportunity to work with a wonderful young woman, *Faith, who was one of seven siblings. Being the eldest, and due to having absent parents, she became the primary caregiver at twelve years old. As you can imagine, being responsible for six lives is no easy feat, especially at such a young age. Because she was busy taking on so many adult roles, she struggled to stay focused in school. The weight of the world was on her shoulders, and the last thing she was worried about was her grades.

After a series of unfortunate events, Faith was moved to her aunt's home. Her aunt cared deeply for her and set her up with a tutor to help her get back on track with schooling. She was now able to focus on her education and learned she actually enjoyed it. She no longer had so many distractions or adult responsibilities, which lifted weight off her shoulders. Faith began to flourish.

Clarissa shared that her increase in self-esteem and confidence was remarkable. "It was a total night and day difference," said Clarissa. Faith was always a loving, kind, and well-behaved young woman, but due to a new environment and increased exposure to opportunities, she was no longer afraid to initiate conversation. She could be herself and focus on her own development as opposed to her six siblings' development. Clarissa shared she was "manicured in a different way": her clothes clean, smile brighter, and energy lighter. She had the ability to learn more about who she was as an individual and began to love herself. She also realized she had someone else who loved her very much—her aunt. For Faith, the exposure to a new way of life with less pressure allowed her the opportunity to spread her wings and take off to a place of self-love and peace.

Sadly, not all girls have the same opportunity to leave toxic environments. As adults, it is important to provide girls who are struggling in school, social situations, and the community with kindness and compassion. Help them see there is hope outside of their home and they are capable of achieving great success in the future.

During Clarissa's job as a college recruiter, she met another wonderful young woman named *Chloe. Chloe was a high school student who was uncertain about what life would look like after graduation. She was a first-generation student and didn't have others to coach her along in her journey. She didn't feel confident in her ability to get into college until she took a bus tour to a nearby college. Clarissa led the way on this trip. The organization Clarissa works for requires students apply for admittance regardless of whether or not they later turn an offer down. Chloe applied and was admitted the same day as the bus trip. She was thrilled! She couldn't believe she got in, and she found out she was eligible for scholarship money. Clarissa noted how she often sees students walk in the door with one belief and walk out the door realizing they have options. Because of this trip, she realized college was a viable option for her. She doubted this to be true prior to this adventure. Just like Faith, there was a new glow to Chloe as a weight was lifted because of the newfound possibilities she discovered.

Another young woman, Lucy, who grew up in Canada, shared about her high school years. She shared about the opportunity she had to grow and flourish in an all-girls high school. She reminisced on the good times she had during the school's weekly Wednesday assemblies. At the assemblies, students had the opportunity to speak and have their voices heard. This helped Lucy build confidence in her public speaking skills. It allowed her and her peers to share excitement about their most recent soccer team wins and the new things they learned on their field trips.

This weekly assembly helped girls to build the skills needed to feel comfortable getting on stage in front of an audience. The stakes didn't feel quite as high because of the overwhelmingly supportive environment. Whether it's speaking at a Wednesday assembly or in front of millions of people in high-profile media appearances, students need adults who will support and help them discover their strengths.

Girls need opportunities. It is our responsibility as adults to help foster these experiences. Moments like speaking in front of her school on Wednesdays helped Lucy realize her teachers cared about her as an individual. She was not just a number. Exploration and exposure help a young girl to gain knowledge, memories, and confidence. **Respect the process: Allow her to discover herself.**

CHAPTER 6

HOW TO: EXPOSURE

———

Education is essential for a young woman's growth. When considering what education is, remember it does not need to be limited to learning that happens in a school building. Education empowers. The United States Agency for International Development states, "When girls are educated, they lead healthier and more productive lives. They gain the skills, knowledge, and self-confidence to escape the cycle of poverty. They become better citizens, parents, and breadwinners. An educated girl has a positive ripple effect on her health, family, community, and society as a whole."[17] This is consistent for girls living in all areas of the world. What is not consistent is access to education. As a school social worker, I will always fight for equity in education as a central task in my career. At the same time, a full analysis of the collective action needed to achieve equity in education is outside the scope of this book. Here, I can share some tangible ways to help expose your girls to new and exciting growth-enhancing opportunities.

---

17 USAID, "Let Girls Learn," *US Agency for International Development*, updated January 26, 2017.

A good education is about so much more than just learning geometry or memorizing dates in history. All of that is important, but an education is also about exploring new things—discovering what makes you come alive, and then being your best at whatever you choose.[18]

—MICHELLE OBAMA

Exposing girls to new experiences is critical in helping them learn about their own passions and strengths. When a girl is passionate and aware of her strengths, she can be unstoppable!

Dr. Damary-Bonilla takes this one step further and explains "exposure equals access." Furthermore, "girls need exposure to mentorship, role models, and opportunities." Unfortunately, just like in the field of education, access to opportunities is often unequal. It's important we, as advocates for young girls, remain aware of these disparities and remove barriers that limit the enriching experiences of youth in marginalized groups. My hope is that you can take advantage of at least one or two ideas here when supporting the girls in your life.

Dr. Damary-Bonilla suggested some fantastic ways to learn about what's going on in the community: attend PTA/PTO or school board meetings, connect with your school guidance

18   Michelle Obama, "Remarks by Mrs. Obama and Madam Kim of the Republic of Korea at a Cultural Event at Annandale High School in Annandale, Virginia," *The American Presidency Project*, October 13, 2011.

counselor or social worker, or attend community-based organizations. I would also suggest joining social networking sites or meetup groups to connect with other parents local to your area.

- Connect with your community: Join the local YMCA, a recreation center, a girls group, or a religious organization. Attend events within the community that are educational or service-based.

It is also important to expose girls to a variety of sports and physical activities at a young age. This will be explored further in the #Sports&Fitness chapter.

- Sporting events: You can go to a major league game or even a neighborhood park to experience the world of sports.

Art is another way girls can be exposed to culture and history—(cough cough) a fun and engaging way to educate!

- Art: Some museums have free days that are open to the public, so give them a call or check online to see when and where you can go. It's also fun to attend plays together, whether that be at the local library, community theater, or on the big stage.

Simply listening to music can also boost a girl's mood and overall health.

- Music: Whether it is attending a big-time concert or hearing a local band doesn't really matter. What matters most is exploring different types of music to see if she might be interested in singing, dancing, or learning to play a new instrument.

In order to afford my immersion trip to Nicaragua during my senior year of undergrad, I chose to fundraise. I was able to raise about half of the funds in order to go with some of my peers. This trip was by far one of the best things I have ever experienced in my life. I not only became more confident in my ability to step outside of my comfort zone, reflect, and be away from home, but I also learned about a whole new way of living. This trip helped me gain an even greater appreciation for cultures that differ from my own. While I highly encourage exposure to opportunities like these for as many girls as possible, it's not necessary to travel outside of the country to learn and grow.

- Trips: Field trips, camp trips, or college trips are all great ways girls can learn more about the big world outside of them. Trips can be expensive, so if you're looking for more affordable ways to make trips a realistic option, consider the following: enrolling her in an organization that supports youth and offers these types of experiences, applying for scholarships, and fundraising.

Exposure can lead to chain reactions that can change the trajectory of a young woman's life. *Jeda's story comes to mind when considering a girl whose confidence increased due to exposure. She was a part of licensed independent social worker Ms. Angela Flowers' girls group. Ms. Flowers took Jeda and the other girls to a shelter where they could give back to the community. They helped serve dinner and spent time with the individuals in the community. When she returned home after the event, she immediately shared with her sister *Monae about one particular individual who enriched her experience. Jeda said that individual proclaimed, "I don't know who you are or what you do, but you're the best thing in life you could ever imagine." Jeda appreciated Ms. Flowers taking her to the shelter. She wouldn't have volunteered at a shelter like that on her own. It helped her to appreciate the blessings in her own life even more.

She started to believe the idea people need to "love me for me." This event inspired her to apply for a Christmas modeling contest through a radio station. Despite having a much curvier figure than her peers, she was determined. Her sister showed her pictures of beautiful plus-size models to demonstrate models come in all shapes and sizes.

After applying, her fears and doubts kicked in. She told Monae if she got a call back, she wouldn't do it. To her surprise, she was selected. She panicked and continued doubting her herself. However, because of the encouragement from her sister and Ms. Flowers reminding her of the growth that can come from doing uncomfortable things and pushing her own limits, she did it. She nailed the photo shoot, and her confidence soared!

Simone Marean shared it's also important when encouraging young women to try new activities we have faith in their ability to meet new people and make new friends. This means we don't always enroll a girl in a new sport or activity only if her friends will join with her. Simone reminds us this can help a girl feel an adult trusts her and her abilities to connect with others. The more she practices connecting with others, the greater her skills and her confidence will become.

Sometimes, taking a trip down the road to a new community is just as important as going halfway across the world. It is possible for communities to look very different even just one or two cities over. As adults, we need to take advantage of these same opportunities to learn about individuals and communities that differ from us so we can consciously empower girls. To this end, exposing a girl to as many things and people as possible helps broaden her perspective and teach her about all of the possibilities in life.

KEY TAKEAWAYS

- Taking risks and trying new things can increase a girl's confidence.
- Expose girls to as many opportunities and experiences as possible. It doesn't have to cost a penny if you get creative!
- Creative fundraising and savvy navigation of community resources may be necessary to increase community access. Not all girls are offered the same opportunities or exposed to the same things in life, and this can impact their ability to see themselves achieving in the future.

Reflection: What are four new activities or experiences I can expose her to this year from the categories in the previous chapter (connect with your community, sporting events, art, music, trips)? What skills or insights can she gain from each of these experiences?

_____

_____

_____

_____

_____

_____

_____

_____

_____

_____

_____

_____

CHAPTER 7

#REPRESENTATION

—

Representation matters. Unfortunately, there is still a clear lack of women in both media and entertainment, as well as in positions of leadership. Even greater is the lack of women of color in these roles. "The lack of representation eats away at [girls'] self-confidence…We know that girls are susceptible to that message. If you can see yourself reflected there is some chance that you can do it. It's very hard just to be told [you] can do it and never see a woman in that role," said Stephanie Hull, president and CEO of Girls Inc.

While some progress has been made, as a society, we still have a long way to go. Here are a few of the many statistics from the Center for American Progress that show the gaps women face in leadership in the United States:

- "In academia, they have earned the majority of doctorates for eight consecutive years but are only 32 percent of full professors and 30 percent of college presidents.
- In the legal profession, they are 45 percent of associates but only 22.7 percent of partners and 19 percent of equity partners.

- As of January 2019, women will represent only 24 percent of members of Congress: 24 percent of the House and 23 percent of the Senate. Women of color represent less than 9 percent of members of Congress.
- As of 2019, 33 of [the top grossing firms] will be led by female CEOs...that sum represents a disproportionately small share of the group as a whole—just 6.6 percent."[19]

These statistics point to areas where girls may fail to see themselves represented in positions of power. But let's not ignore other factors, such as lack of female representation of various shapes, sizes, colors, and cultures when discussing this topic.

While there is a lack of representation, there is not a lack of amazing women who possess the skills to be successful in these roles. Many brilliant and inspiring young women are leading the way for future generations, working to break down some of these barriers.

Rehana Paul, an eighteen-year-old Indian American woman, founded *Overachiever Magazine* at the age of sixteen. According to her website, "Our name is poking fun at the stereotype that all Asians are overachievers, especially Asian women. It's also in recognition of all the Asian women who have had no choice but to be overachievers: managing societal expectations, family obligations, and educational opportunities, all while fighting the patriarchy." Asian women from all around the world can contribute their thoughts and feelings

19   Judith Warner, Nora Ellmann, Diana Boesch, "The Women's Leadership Gap," *Center for American Progress*, November, 20 2018.

about these types of issues on this site. Part of the inspiration behind *Overachiever Magazine* was Rehana's own struggle with self-esteem and confidence in her younger years. She mentioned math and science were never a strong suit for her, which was tough because of the stereotypes and expectations they brought upon her.

Because of the lack of Indian American role models who excelled in the social sciences, she always felt as though her passions and talents were not valid. "Stereotypes can be a nasty thing," exclaimed Rehana, "especially in regards to the impact they can have on a girl's confidence." Here is where society has it backwards; rather than praising and encouraging girls to be who they want to be and empowering them to embrace their individuality, they are confined to a small box in which they can achieve. Recognition is often only given to girls if they fit in that small and often uncomfortable box. So, as caring adults, we must also encourage them to break outside of it by being bold and walking down uncharted territories. As Rehana said, we must teach girls to "aim bigger and tell them they can do it."

Rehana also pointed out that while growing up she realized being confident was not always seen as a positive quality, but rather as arrogance and a form of bragging. She highlighted the clear-cut difference between the way many boys and girls are treated in her culture. More specifically, girls are meant to "help in kitchen and clean, while boys have the luxury of chilling and playing video games." A girl's goal should be to aspire to marriage by her mid-twenties. Due to the caste system in India, prior to being married, women in a higher caste may have greater opportunities to be more highly educated compared to their peers. The families they are marrying into appreciate when their future daughter-in-law is well-educated.

However, the expectation she will remove the majority of focus from her own career to place it on others can distort a girl's confidence. Rehana mentioned she often witnesses females in her culture focus on being good daughters, sisters, and future wives, while boys seemingly get praised for the bare minimum. Sadly, this can have a real blow to the way a girl feels about herself and her abilities to maintain balance and achieve both inside and outside of the home. Perhaps this is why so many of the girls she interviews for internships lack confidence in themselves.

Rehana spoke about one particular girl, *Prisha, who came into the interview trembling. She even stuttered as she shared her name. As she spoke about her previous accomplishments, she was unable to confidently speak about her experiences. Instead, she put herself down. She said her position as a camp counselor was nothing special. Let me tell you: Being a camp counselor can be tough! While Prisha stumbled through her interview, Rehana gave her a chance to join the team because sometimes the key to unleashing young women's superpowers is simply believing in them. By the end of her internship, Prisha felt accomplished. She was able to share about the amazing work she did during her semester that helped Asian women embrace their individuality all around the world. She helped them have a voice and raise one another up. Just like Rehana, Prisha realized the "model minority myth" is just that: a myth. All girls have strengths and weaknesses. Some are good at math and science while others struggle. However, the grade on a piece of paper does not define a woman's worth.

There is inaccuracy in the "model minority" label, which is what Rehana's site is working to eliminate. The model minority stereotype is all Asians are extremely smart, particularly in science, technology, engineering, and mathematics (STEM). It has also been said Asian children have "tiger moms," or moms who are strict and demanding. It is considered a myth because Asian Americans are not a homogeneous group. This means culture and ethnicity vary from one region to another. Therefore, it is virtually impossible to apply this label to all Asian Americans and capture all of their distinctive experiences.[20]

Rehana is beyond grateful for the community she has because of *Overachiever Magazine*. Prior to founding this magazine, she lacked an essential element to helping a young girl build confidence: a strong community of other women and girls. Growing up, she didn't see many women in her culture supporting one another. It all came back to that idea of the model minority. In other words, she was taught life was about competition with others and being the best. Over time, she realized having a community of women who support one another is both important to her own growth and to the growth of females in society as a whole. We must teach girls from a young age that while there is a time and space for healthy competition, there is also a great need to collaborate with peers and support one another.

---

20 Frieda Wong and Richard Halgin, "The 'Model Minority': Bane or Blessing for Asian Americans?" *Journal of Multicultural Counseling and Development* 34, no.1 (January 2006): 38–49.

It was neat not only to be able to talk to the founder of *Overachiever Magazine*, Rehana, but also to a fifteen-year-old contributor, Mariam. Mariam was born in the United Kingdom and spent the greater majority of her life growing up in Qatar. Being one of the few girls of color in her school in the United Kingdom, she sometimes felt as though her voice did not matter. I frequently witnessed girls of color feeling less than—because of their uniqueness—as a common theme throughout interviews conducted for this book.

Even worse, microaggressions from others penetrate these wounds deeper. A microaggression is when someone intentionally or unintentionally uses a prejudicial or derogatory statement or action towards a marginalized group or individual within that group.

Here are a few examples:

- "I'm not racist, I have several (insert racial background) friends."
- "Where are you from?" "I'm from America…" "No, but really, where are you from?"
- "When I look at you, I don't see color."
- Following a person of color around a store to "make sure they don't steal."

Mariam shared an example from her own life. Growing up, her teachers would assume she could not speak English. They would say to her, "Mariam, your English is so good." (This comment is a microaggression.) Her teachers often assumed she was not as smart as her white peers, which was not the case. Despite her efforts to ignore these rude and ignorant comments, they still had a negative impact on her self-esteem. Feeling different from all of her friends sometimes led to an even worse feeling of isolation.

Because of the sore lack of representation she had growing up, Mariam agrees it is crucial girls have some role models who look like them. As adults, we must find ways to highlight diverse women who are confident, strong, and successful. Mariam proclaimed, "My confidence increases when I see people who look like me, are from my ethnic background, and are represented in the media. Having them in powerful, competent positions makes me feel like I can do that too."

Women can be heroes. In fact, one of the activities I conduct during Empowered & Poised programming is called "super sheroes." This activity helps girls realize it isn't just men who are heroes. It allows them to recognize and celebrate their strengths in a variety of areas. Girls will share how they are sheroes at home, in school, in their communities, and in other areas of their lives. Allowing girls to harness their potential from a young age will help them grow into self-assured women who can be role models for generations to come.

Thankfully, there has been some progress towards seeing sheroes in the media. "Hero" powers such as superhuman strength, fighting abilities, competing, and winning are traits typically associated with masculinity. Traditionally feminine traits like compassion, gentleness, and connectedness can also be celebrated as superpowers. A few names that often come to the top of people's minds are Supergirl, Wonder Woman, Mother Teresa, and Malala Yousafzai.

One simple way you can help your girls learn about successful women, or sheroes, from various backgrounds is to encourage reading. You can read your daughters a variety of books that highlight girls and women from different backgrounds at a young age. From there, encourage them to seek out additional media sources that highlight successful women. Girls need role models. We need to be role models for them. We need to advocate for greater representation of women in media. Period.

CHAPTER 8

HOW TO: REPRESENTATION

———

She must see it to believe it. Girls need to see people who look like them in a variety of roles. While, as adults, we know a young woman is capable even without having visible role models, young women can struggle to recognize this reality, especially if we aren't engaging in meaningful conversations with them.

One particular example that stood out to me was one Dr. Rome shared about a time a doctor of color had to step away from her primary care role. In response, one of her eight-year-old patients' mothers proclaimed, "I want you to still be our doctor. You're the first doctor who actually looks like my daughter." This mother understood the concept of representation. It was important her daughter had examples of successful women. We must make conscious choices regarding who surrounds our children.

Another area where there is a great need for representation is among teachers. Think back to the first time you had a person of color or man as a teacher. For many, this did not happen until later in life, and for some, it may have never happened at all. Dr. Alexander shared when she first started teaching in higher education. On the first day of class, Dr. Alexander patiently waited for her class to arrive. Prior to class starting, many of her students spoke to her as if she was another student. They proceeded to share with her, "I heard the professor is nice but gives a lot of work." Once class began, she admitted to her students she was, in fact, the instructor. This led to a great discussion about the reasons why they might have thought she couldn't be the professor. Thankfully, this class was focused on diversity, so it fit right into the curriculum.

We need to help girls realize there is power in representation, breaking down stereotypes, and moving away from comparison. Unfortunately, the images of female representation most often seen by girls in advertising and the media are *designed* to look nothing like most women. The overwhelmingly white, thin, carefully curated representation in the media fuels a fierce culture of self-criticism, comparison, and competitiveness among young women. Ann Klotz, headmistress at Laurel School (a school for girls), believes "comparison is the thief of joy." This could not be truer. Conversations can help change our thoughts and attitudes.

In 1988, Carol Gilligan was the first individual to report on the decline in confidence in preteen girls due to a shift in placing their self-worth on appearance and weight. She suggested, "[Girls' confidence drops] because of the widening gap between girls' self-images and society's messages about what girls should be like."[21]

While social media has some positive benefits, it can also cause a girl to dismiss her own strengths and experiences when she is constantly seeing lives that seem so glamorous compared to her own. Oftentimes, social media depicts "confident girls" as traveling the world on their own, wearing the hottest designer trends, and showing off their seemingly perfect bodies. However, none of this directly correlates to actually being confident, nor is it realistically attainable for all girls, or even most girls.

Despite widespread awareness about how embellished media can be, girls still desire to look like the individuals they see. In fact, a national media study found "[one in three girls] changed something about their appearance to resemble [a] character [they wanted to look like on TV]."[22] Therefore, it is important when watching television, scrolling through social media, and taking in pop culture we help our girls become conscious consumers.

Klotz suggests helping girls to improve their skills in media literacy. She shared when a song comes on, you can ask questions to young women like, "What do you think about the way that singer characterizes women?" You can also engage in conversations regarding advertising and media,

---

21 Carol Gilligan, *Mapping the Moral Domain: A Contribution of Women's Thinking to Psychological Theory and Education* (Center for the Study of Gender, Education and Human Development, Harvard University Graduate School of Education, 1998).

22 "Media and Girls," MediaSmarts, August 22, 2014.

and why certain images or products might sell better or become more popular than others. Media can include print, Internet, broadcasting, games, and movies. Help girls begin thinking critically about where there are the biggest gaps in representation and why. How can we make the media we consume more inclusive of a wider range of body types and human experiences?

The following are a few suggestions for ways you can expand representation and reduce comparison:

- Bring a variety of speakers from different professions and cultures into the classroom.
- Encourage girls to explore books that represent diverse backgrounds and experiences.
- Watch movies in class and as a family that mirror your experience, as well as differ from it.
- Remind girls confidence and beauty come in all different shapes and sizes.
- Help girls learn how to limit or carefully curate the media they see. You can encourage girls to unfollow accounts the second they begin to make them feel insecure or when they recognize they are comparing themselves.

What we see in the media largely impacts what we believe we are capable of achieving. If there is an area that lacks representation, inspire and motivate her to find her strength from within to be a leader and change the future for girls who come after her. You can teach her about women like Amelia Earhart (1932: first woman to pilot, solo, a nonstop flight across the Atlantic Ocean), Katharine Graham (1972:

first woman to be a Fortune 500 CEO—CEO of *The Washington Post*), Junko Tabei (1975: first woman to summit Mount Everest), and Aretha Franklin (1987: first woman inducted into the Rock and Roll Hall of Fame). These women were all trailblazers in their own way. It may be difficult to find a role model in the exact field a girl is aspiring to achieve; however, if you introduce her to other strong women who led the way, perhaps she will see herself in them.

Klotz reminds us girls often have a "burning commitment to make world better" and "youth [have] energy and power we must never forget." Helping girls become conscious consumers of media can help their self-esteem and confidence, as well as inspire future generations. They can pass along their newfound insights to their younger siblings and maybe even their own children one day.

"Girls need fearless, visible role models, starting from a very young age, to foster greater awareness of the possibilities in their own lives and help them discover their own brilliant paths. The best role models for girls are the ones they see every day: at school on the playground, in the advanced calculus and physics courses, in the art studio, on the theater stage, at swim practice, at Girl Scout meetings, and on the robotics team," says executive director of National Coalition of Girls' Schools Megan Murphy. Make it a priority to ensure young girls have strong role models both in real life and in the media.

KEY TAKEAWAYS

- Open up conversations to help girls become conscious consumers of media.
- Offer suggestions of media (books, movies, social sites, etc.) that are representative of her and her background.
- Help girls find both present-day and historical individuals they can admire and emulate.

Reflection: How do I currently make representation a priority in my own life? How and where can I introduce more diversity, representation, and inclusion in her life?

_____

_____

_____

_____

_____

_____

_____

_____

_____

_____

_____

_____

CHAPTER 9

#AFFIRMATIONS

———

We must empower our girls through positive affirmations. Even more importantly, we must teach them how to self-affirm. According to researchers Cohen and Sherman, "Self-affirmation [is] an act that manifests one's adequacy and thus affirms one's sense of global self-integrity...[Affirmations] bring about a more expansive view of the self and its resources."[23] For the purpose of this book, affirmations can be an act or encouraging phrase that elicits positive thoughts and feelings. It can be a hug, high five, thumbs-up, or positive statement.

Stating positive mantras may impact an individual's self-esteem and confidence if done properly. Are you wondering how to do this? Here's the key: **Affirmations must reflect personal values.** Values can be conceptual, like respect, responsibility, or hard work. They can also be concrete, like education, religion, or importance placed on spending time with family. If you don't believe it, it won't work. Therefore,

---

23   Geoffrey L. Cohen & David K. Sherman, "The Psychology of Change: Self-Affirmation and Social Psychological Intervention," *Annual Review of Psychology* 65, no.1 (2014): 337.

affirmations must be both positive and focus on actions that can be taken which align with one's strengths, true self, and values. They should be "positively focused and targeted at actions you can take to reinforce your sense of self-identity."[24]

Referring to the impact of affirmations on the brain, Christopher Cascio, PhD, writes, "Affirmation takes advantage of our reward circuits, which can be quite powerful. Many studies have shown that these circuits can do things like dampen pain and help us maintain balance in the face of threats."[25] For girls, threats could include stressors like academic pressure or relational conflict. "There is MRI evidence suggesting that certain neural pathways are increased when people practice self-affirmation tasks...the ventromedial prefrontal cortex—involved in positive valuation and self-related information processing—becomes more active when we consider our personal values."[26] In other words, it is scientifically proven there is a physical change in the brain that occurs from using affirmations that are linked to personal values.

Meredith Ellis, MEd, drew from her experiences as a school counselor and teen-life skills program facilitator when asked the question: "What is your best advice for individuals who work and live with girls on how they can help them build their confidence?"

---

24 Catherine Moore, "Positive Daily Affirmations: Is There Science Behind It?" PositivePsychology.com, January 30, 2021.

25 "Study Reveals the Neural Mechanics of Self-Affirmation," Annenberg School for Communication, November 20, 2015.

26 Ibid.

She shared, "Helping girls clearly identify their thoughts and emotions can be powerful. Teen girls' automatic thoughts are often self-critical and focused on perceived personal deficits. These thoughts might sound like 'Calm down! You're laughing too loud' or 'You shouldn't be angry. This isn't a big deal.' Often, girls (and people generally) have no idea how unsupportive and insensitive their internal self-talk really sounds.

If we, as adults, can take a truly open, nonjudgmental approach to asking girls specific questions like 'what thoughts were going through your head when that happened?' and 'what was your first thought when she made that comment?' we can help girls recognize and examine unnecessary cruelty in their self-talk. We can encourage girls to treat themselves with more compassion by responding to their critical thoughts with 'it sounds like that was really painful for you' or 'it sounds like you were really trying to do the right thing.'"

When girls are in pain, helping them connect to what they are feeling (anger, fear, grief), rather than what they think they should be feeling (easygoing joy, concern for others), is key. Girls frequently learn they should first strive to make others comfortable, which often requires sacrificing their own comfort. In other words, being a "good girl" is often presented as synonymous with being accommodating and having few, if any, personal needs or demands. For this reason, girls often chastise themselves for emotions that could inconvenience or displease others.

Girls are too often indirectly affirmed for keeping the peace—as opposed to advocating for their own ideas or needs—when they hear comments like "she never complains" or "she's always so happy!" It's our job to affirm girls' experiences of less beloved emotions. Helping young women develop confidence means teaching them to honor all of their internal experiences with self-compassion. Sometimes being less likable to others makes us more likable to ourselves.

Yang, a Chinese woman who moved to the United States at age sixteen, described how she was fortunate to have a father who always uplifted her and wasn't concerned with her fitting into society's mold. He was constantly encouraging her throughout her younger years. This served as a protective factor to the external environment in China. Yang stated, "In China, by the time you are in middle school, girls are pretty much expected to be failing in math and science." She believes constantly hearing phrases like this largely contributes to the lack of women in STEM.

Edutopia shared an article called "Keeping Girls in STEM: 3 Barriers, 3 Solutions," which explained that as girls progress in school, the gender gap increases in participation of STEM courses. Issues of race and class only further compound this issue. The article continued, "When girls become aware through both subtle and overt cultural messages about male superiority in math, it makes each encounter with math and technology more fraught, triggering self-doubt in even the most studious young girls."[27]

Fortunately for Yang, her father believed in her and her abilities, even in these areas. He made it clear she could be

---

27   Carly Berwick, "Keeping Girls in STEM: 3 Barriers, 3 Solutions," Edutopia, George Lucas Educational, March 12, 2019.

successful despite society's expectations for girls to fall behind. Now, Yang is a successful woman in the field of finance, and she sees very few women of color among her in her field.

While Yang remembers too-low expectations placed on girls' STEM abilities, she also remembers the pressure society put on her to look a certain way. She shared that beauty standards in her culture compelled girls to desire lighter skin, thinner figures, wider eyes, and the "perfect" nose. Some of her friends began utilizing "beauty" products and having cosmetic surgeries as early as age thirteen. She vividly remembers her friends struggling with body image and lacking confidence because of the pressure they felt to meet society's expectations of what they should look like. While her mother was generally an advocate for her, Yang reminisced about a time her mom's words stung. It was summer, and she was enjoying most of her days in the sunshine playing soccer. She had always been an athlete and possessed an athletic body, which was not seen as the ideal for girls in her culture. She developed a love for soccer at a young age and continued to spend her time kicking around a ball, despite the fact this further sculpted her body. It is possible her father's love and affirmations played a role in her ability to overcome external pressures to conform to beauty ideals.

During this same summer, due to the sun, her skin had a glow to it. She became what is considered "a bronzed beauty" in some cultures—but not her own. Her mother was furious with her and yelled at her for getting so dark. This experience reinforced her belief that, if she was not light enough, she was not good enough. We must be careful about what we say to girls and how we say it. The narratives we share with them, through our behaviors and our words, can have lifelong impacts that help to build or break their confidence.

The Encyclopedia of Adolescence points out, "Self-affirmation during adolescence obviously can have many positive consequences, and likewise if an adolescent feels less affirmed in their sense of self, they are more likely to experience negative consequences."[28] In Yang's case, the stereotypes about girls in China being inferior to boys in STEM subjects and needing to be lighter-skinned were capable of threatening her identity as a whole.

With this being said, it's important to also remind yourself no parent is the perfect parent. No teacher is the perfect teacher. No person is the perfect person. So, while Yang's mother yelled at her daughter out of anger, this does not mean she was a bad mother. In fact, Yang spoke extremely highly of her mother. She shared that her mother was loving, supportive, and advocated for individuals from all backgrounds. Yang's mom supported her in every way she knew how throughout her childhood and adolescent years; however, good parents and supportive adults can fall victim to restrictive beliefs about girls' appearance and behavior, just as girls do.

If, as an adult, you catch yourself in a sticky situation where you weren't quite the model a young woman needed, be kind to yourself. Remind yourself it is okay to make mistakes. Positively affirming our girls must start with positively affirming ourselves. Everyone makes mistakes. Say to yourself, "I

---

28 Encyclopedia of Adolescence, s.v., "Affirmation," by Roger J.R. Levesque, February 28, 2018.

make mistakes, but I am not my mistakes. My mistakes do not define me."

We must also be brave enough to set our own egos aside and apologize. Apologizing to girls helps them see it is okay not to be perfect. When girls realize trying is the best we can do sometimes, it gives them permission to make their own mistakes. When girls see all humans are imperfect, it can help them have more realistic expectations of themselves. Thus, a girl's self-esteem will likely increase because she will not have set the bar so high that her goals are unattainable. This also helps girls recognize they deserve an apology from individuals who hurt them or made them feel less than valuable. Adults who treat everyone with respect prove to be strong role models.

Girls can begin to realize their worth from the examples we set, which includes speaking kindly to ourselves and others. No one should have to look, act, or sound a certain way to be valuable and treated kindly. We must consciously empower girls in our actions and words, ensuring the affirmations we offer align with the values of each individual.

CHAPTER 10

HOW TO: AFFIRMATIONS

———

Did you know not all affirmations are equally as helpful? "Empowerment of girls isn't simply slogans, such as 'You go, girl!' or 'Girl power!' although slogans can help to build solidarity and to lend special support. Empowerment for girls means an assessment of their collective and individual strengths. For the psychotherapist, it means understanding a specific girl's strengths within the context of her family and her community."[29]

Angela Flowers, licensed independent social worker, is a pro when it comes to helping girls discover their strengths. She has also developed a curriculum for a girls group called DIVAS, which encourages them to identify five positive strengths before and after their participation to measure increases in their confidence. Using affirmations that are specific empowers young women to identify strengths within themselves. Ms. Flowers mentioned at the beginning of group many girls struggle with social skills like eye contact and

---

29 Norine Johnson, "On Treating Adolescent Girls: Focus on Strengths and Resiliency in Psychotherapy," *Journal of Clinical Psychology* 59, no. 11 (November 2003): 1194.

cannot identify five strengths. By the end of the program, girls can identify what assets they possess.

It is important we help girls to focus on their internal strengths, such as their sense of humor, connection to meaningful aspects of their heritage, and compassion for others. We must shift focus from external qualities, like fame, status, or beauty, to internal qualities.

One way you can help a girl identify her values and interests is through affirming her personal, racial, and cultural identity. Marissa Buendicho highlighted the importance of being culturally sensitive, or being aware of the impact culture and history has on individuals. Again, she reminds us of the importance of affirming girls and their backgrounds in the following story she shared.

She treated a young woman named *Ciara during her time working for a group psychotherapy practice. Ciara's background was denigrated during school by her peers. Her teacher failed to speak up and out against the injustice she was experiencing. Ciara mentioned to Marissa she did not want to "feel sensitive." As a result, Marissa chose to help her learn about her cultural history, intersectionality, and what these meant to her. In working with Marissa, she realized it is okay to feel anger, sadness, and any other emotions that arise as a result of facing racism and sexism.

Marissa equated the stages Ciara went through to the stages of grief. Marissa stated, "She was grieving who she once was in terms of the racism and sexism she experienced and not really saying anything. [She moved] into a new stage of development of speaking up for herself and learning how to adjust the volume…" Shortly after finishing her sessions with Marissa, Ciara was planning on moving from Hawaii back to the continental United States. She shared with Marissa she was going to become an activist so she could speak up and out against the injustices other women like her face. Ciara transformed from feeling like she did not have permission to get mad about painfully enduring the racial slurs of her classmates to becoming a courageous leader in her community. This story highlights the importance of affirming girls in both their feelings and their backgrounds. We do not have to have the same background as an individual to allow them to express themselves and explore their values.

Another way to support girls in developing their values is to encourage them to volunteer in their community. Dr. Rome recognizes it is empowering for young people to feel like part of the solution rather than part of the problem. When they give back, they begin to see themselves as "valid, visible, and appreciated."

She mentioned that in her experience, young ladies who get the most out of their bat mitzvah (the religious initiation ceremony for a Jewish girl) take part in some sort of community service project. This can teach young people to give from the heart. Community service projects help "feed the soul in the process to adulthood." These young women put hard work and effort into their projects, which often helps them to feel accomplished and proud. Often, commending them on a job well done after they have devoted great time and efforts into their projects can help to boost their spirits.

Growing up, I volunteered in a variety of areas, including with Meals on Wheels, at vacation Bible school, and at the local concession stands. I remember feeling a sense of satisfaction, as Dr. Rome had mentioned. I was happy to know I could give back to my community, even at a young age. These types of activities helped me feel a sense of purpose and connection to others. When we feel connected to our communities and believe we can make a difference, our confidence increases.

Therefore, we must help girls recognize they are capable by gathering evidence to support the verbal affirmations we share with them. This evidence could be the internal work they have done to recognize their strengths and understand more about their historical roots or outwardly making a difference in the community. Consider searching the Internet using the phrase "list of values." Work with the girl in your life to determine the top five values that rank highest as priorities for her and her life.

HERE ARE SOME GUIDELINES FOR GIVING POWERFUL AFFIRMATIONS TO GIRLS:

- Be specific.
  - Patrice, I noticed you passed the ball to three other girls during the final quarter. I bet it helped Suzie make the basket. You're such a good teammate!
- Focus on internal qualities.
  - I noticed you have been using your art supplies. I am so impressed by your creativity and dedication to drawing!

- Focus on personal strengths. (If she is clearly not skilled in an area, do not offer empty praise. She will see right through this.)
  - You bring so much to our family by speaking your mind. I love you can clearly tell me how you're feeling, even if it's hard for me to hear. Have you ever considered joining the debate team? I think you'd be really good!
- Focus on progress—not perfection. (Avoid using the word "perfect" to affirm her.)
  - Mary, I'm so proud of you. I can tell your hard work is really paying off! I saw on your behavior chart this week you raised your hand three times more than last week.

Ultimately, it is our responsibility to help girls develop a sense of agency. This means we help girls become aware they have the power to make a difference in their communities and the world. We must give girls the opportunity and encouragement to try and choose.

KEY TAKEAWAYS
- Help girls develop their values and strengths and incorporate these when affirming them or having them develop self-affirmations.
- Utilize conscious empowerment as a way for girls to affirm who they authentically are: race, culture, religious background, sexual orientation, ability, and all!
- Encourage activities like volunteerism, where girls can realize it's not just a cliché to say, "It is in giving that we receive."

Reflection: What are one to three ways I can make the statements more meaningful when I affirm her (e.g., using her name, focusing on internal qualities, incorporating her strengths, focusing on progress over perfection)? Practice writing out a positive affirmation based on what you've learned in the past two chapters.

_____

_____

_____

_____

_____

_____

_____

_____

_____

_____

_____

CHAPTER 11

#BESEEN

What does being seen mean? Often, when we think of "being seen" as a female, it means lighting up the room. While there is nothing wrong with turning heads, to #BeSeen also means having the courage to show people your authentic self. This may look like being proud of your intelligence, being goofy and allowing people to see your silly side, or getting angry when you have been treated poorly. It is showing the real, raw, vulnerable, authentic you. To help a girl #BeSeen, it is important to help her understand it is okay if not everyone likes her.

My little sister Darian posted a quote on her Twitter that I loved. It said, "You can be the juiciest, ripest peach in the world, and there's still going to be someone who doesn't like peaches." That is the unfortunate truth. There will always be something someone doesn't like about each of us. Despite this reality, we must help young women love and embrace their authentic selves. We should be allowed to #BeSeen in all of our states, whether we are dressed up and glamorous or just had a rough day with eyes puffy from tears streaming down our faces.

All too often, girls are taught to be quiet, polite, proper, and have it "together." In fact, a study on the development on feminine norms highlighted that throughout history, femininity has been measured on characteristics like being nice, focusing on relationships, being attractive, being thin, nurturing others, being silent, deferring to men, and being domestic.[30] These expectations imposed on girls tend to limit their confidence in their rights to assert themselves, speak up, and be seen. For this reason, confidence must be nourished in girls just like any other skill.

Lou Bergholz, author of *Vital Connections*, is a phenomenal male role model for young women. The world needs men like Lou, because the way men and boys treat girls as adolescents often shapes their views on how they should be treated as they become women. We must make sure young women are exposed to positive opportunities and people. Lou shared, "It's a muscle. Confidence: It's a muscle. It's a skill. Everybody has it. Most children have it when they're tiny, but it gets crushed out of them in very, very big ways…" Not only does he strongly believe in the importance of connecting with youth, he lives and breathes this type of work. He reenergizes youth so they can piece together the parts of their confidence that have been distorted by social pressures.

Lou spent three years working in the Gaza territory of Palestine. He had the opportunity to get to know *Ghada. Ghada, in her early twenties, was slightly older than the participants she worked with. She was struggling with confidence that

---

30   James R. Mahalik et al., "Development of the Conformity to Feminine Norms Inventory," *Sex Roles* 52, no. 7 (April 2005): 417–435.

resulted from a serious accident a few years prior. She disclosed she was a burn survivor. Her burns covered her from head to toe.

Some Muslim women choose to wear burqas (a semi-sheer veil which covers the face and body). Burqas are often worn for reasons such as averting male gazes or retaining modesty. For Ghada, she found solace in wearing a burqa because there was no judgement or fear of her burns being seen. She felt Empowered by having control over who she showed her burns to and from whom she hid them. She was ashamed of her burns and was the frequent subject of town gossip. She lived in a small community, so everyone knew her as "the girl who got burned." It even caused individuals to assume she was incapable.

For instance, in her interview to be a mentor for a youth-based program, she wasn't listed as a top-sixteen choice by anyone except Lou. Lou could see through her insecurities. She was savvy, had intelligent answers to the questions she was asked, and possessed an extremely warm and loving heart for children. He believed in her. She was going to be great, and he could sense that. But when a girl's confidence is low, she is often overlooked and seen as incapable. Lou recognized her experiences had given her wisdom and could help the students in the program. Her story made her relatable, and she could impact students in the greatest of ways. So, he fought hard to keep her on board and give her a chance to shine. After much discussion and debate, the organization brought her on the team.

A little more than a month into the project, Ghada entered a small house that had been converted to a community center for after-school activities. She rolled in and put her bag down. Then, the room fell silent. Ghada took off her burqa, keeping her hijab (hair covering) on. Never before had she taken it off outside of her own home. She confidently said to her colleagues and the participants, "I can't encourage you to be yourself here if I can't be myself. I want you to accept me for who I am." And they did just that. They accepted her for who she was: a beautiful, warm, and confident woman. Her face was glowing. She no longer felt the need to hide.

This program helped to glue back the pieces of her confidence that were shattered. Her confidence was shattered not because of the literal burns, but because of the scars that nasty and negative comments can have on a girl. Not only did Ghada's own confidence grow, but she showed the students what being a true hero can look like. She was a model for them and affirmed them in the same way they affirmed her.

Fast forward a few years; now, Lou has a beautiful little girl of his own. From birth, he and his wife have given their daughter permission to express herself fully. They let her know she is allowed to get loud, live large, and take control of her own life. While nature plays a role in the development of a young woman, Lou feels strongly most things are learned. In other words, effort and practice are essential in helping girls become confident.

Since parents and educators cannot do everything, the things we can do for girls have the power to create lifelong impacts.

Lou emphasized the importance of honoring his daughter's first 'no' and respecting her boundaries. Many of you reading this book may be past the point of a first 'no,' however, better late than never! Here's what I mean: When a girl says no, she deserves to be respected. If she doesn't want to hug everybody in the family, she shouldn't be forced. Instead, she can wave, give a high five, or share a fist bump. Teaching girls about boundaries and *respecting the boundaries girls set with us* can help them gain the confidence to take control of their well-being. It shouldn't take saying it five times for the word "stop" to be heard and honored.

Lou shared, "We do a terrible thing to kids. We tickle in the morning, and they say 'no.' But, they're laughing. So, we tickle again and again. Then, about five times later, you can tell they don't like it, so we stop. We do this with kissing, hugging, and squeezing. This isn't treating young people with the respect, space, or boundaries that they deserve. Actions like this quickly translate from your parents doing this to somebody else doing it. It takes someone saying 'no' five times before anyone believes you. But, more importantly, before you believe yourself." Lou knows that one 'no' should be enough, which is why he and his wife are ensuring their daughter knows this too. "For a young woman to be able to know that one 'no' is all it takes. Anything more than that is complete disrespect and violation. I desperately want my daughter to believe that everyone matters." We must assist girls in believing in their own power by affirming their boundaries.

While he admittedly still has a lot of learning to do when it comes to raising a girl, Lou is confident "no means no" is something all girls need to learn. He also highlighted the importance of letting her know it's okay to take up space and have her voice be heard. It is a priority his daughter learns from a young age how powerful her body is by allowing her to move, break, and build things.

From Lou to all individuals working with girls: "Let her be loud. Let her voice ring and shout and not worry about who hears it, for all the reasons that it gives you confidence, but also because it's a lifesaving skill."

Lou's passion for implementing the phrase "no means no" in his own household stems from his experience with the organization and founder of No Means No Kenya and IMpower United, Lee Paiva. "No Means No Worldwide is a global rape prevention organization whose mission is to end sexual violence against women and children…[Their] research shows an average 50 percent decrease in the incidence of sexual assault for girls taught IMpower (a type of self-defense). Girls learn to identify risk, say 'no,' and talk their way out of trouble. If that 'no' is not respected, they also learn physical skills to back it up."[31] A large part of self-defense is poise—"a key component in equality and empowerment." Paiva, like many others interviewed, shared she believes in teaching girls skills—skills that can help them learn how to use their voice, raise their hand, not worry about being "too much" of anything, and stand up for what they believe in. She believes in the power of girls and giving them the skills to know if anything gets in their way, they can overcome it. "Confidence comes when you have skills, when you feel capable."

---

31 "About," No Means No Worldwide, accessed February 7, 2021.

We must teach girls how to #BeSeen in ways that are different from how we currently view girls. We must help them understand being the "prettiest, nicest, or happiest" girl in the room may not equate to being their best self. We need to embrace girls' uniqueness, teach them "no means no," and help them realize they are capable of stepping up and out to let their voice be proudly heard.

CHAPTER 12

HOW TO: BE SEEN

Famous American professor, lecturer, author, and podcast host Brené Brown proclaimed, "Courage starts with showing up and letting ourselves be seen."[32] It can be scary to be vulnerable and let our guards down. As I mentioned earlier, writing this book is real and raw for me. It's been a very vulnerable journey. I also feel courageous for taking this step in faith. We need to encourage all girls to be courageous and be seen.

Girls have different interests. Embrace her individuality. Regardless of if she ends up loving sports, band, theater, art, or another form of expression, help her cultivate skills in the area where she feels best. Try not to deter her from where her passions lie because of biases you hold in your own life. For example, some people may believe certain sports are not for girls, like boxing or rugby. If she enjoys it, support her and help her become the best she can!

---

32 Brené Brown, *Daring Greatly: How the Courage to Be Vulnerable Transforms the Way We Live, Love, Parent, and Lead* (London, UK: Penguin Random House Audio Publishing Group, 2011).

One way we can help support the girls in our lives is by taking a look at our own biases. If we are going to ask girls to do the tough work necessary to build their own confidence, we need to do the tough work to better understand ourselves. The first step is to simply become aware of the biases we hold. As mentioned in the previous chapter, there are many feminine norms imposed upon us. Do you believe girls should only participate in certain activities or act in certain ways? Would it bother you if a girl didn't want to wear a dress to a fancy function? How about if she wanted to join the wrestling team? Would you be proud of your daughter for wanting to be a construction worker?

Trust me, there are certain areas in which I have really needed to look at myself and ask these same questions. One of my good friends mentioned her daughter wanted to join the wrestling team. She seemed to have no issues with it. I, on the other hand, had to really consider whether or not this was something I would feel comfortable with if I had a daughter of my own. If you are feeling slightly uncomfortable or uncertain about how you might answer, you are not alone. With the constant influx of messages about how women and girls should be, it can be challenging to not only accept but embrace individuals who don't fit into the mold society has built. This is exactly why, as adults, we must take a look at ourselves and become the models girls need us to be. We need to work diligently to shed our own rigid feminine expectations because, even as adults, this can be challenging.

Think about all the times girls are taught they should be celebrated for being nice, small, and modest. Many Disney movies are great examples. Nearly every princess is petite, flawlessly gorgeous, sings sweet songs, and is saved by a man. Even Mulan, arguably one of the strongest princesses, had to become a man in order to be respected. Thankfully, more recent heroines like Moana and Elsa depict courageous, independent women who don't need to be saved, rescued, or even have a romantic plot line at all.

As you begin questioning the stereotypes and norms pressed upon women and girls, ask yourself if you are unconsciously guiding girls toward conforming to these norms. You can ask yourself questions like, "Do I not want my daughter to do this because it's not seen as nice, modest, or ladylike?" If the answer is yes, you may want to reconsider allowing her to try that activity. It may give her the opportunity to express a new and important part of herself.

Similar questions can be asked when helping guide girls in their relationships. All too often, girls are taught to please others. Girls are taught to please their friends, significant others, and even strangers. We need to become more comfortable with giving girls permission to have boundaries and permission to walk away when relationships are not comfortable or no longer serve them. Allow them to stand up for themselves instead of pushing them to make up with a friend. Just as it's okay for adults to walk away from a career that no longer serves them, it's okay for girls to walk away from areas of their life that aren't helpful to their own growth. It is possible to teach girls to be kind and advocate for themselves at the same time.

One story that comes to mind is a young woman who I worked with for a few years, *Rebecca. Rebecca's mother constantly interfered in her daughter's relationships, assuming she knew best. She loved one of her daughter's friends, so when they had a falling out, she encouraged Rebecca to make up with her. However, Rebecca had little desire to spend time with this friend. She shared with me she didn't enjoy spending time with her anymore and she'd rather hang out with her new friend, *Emily. She and Emily had a lot more in common now, as girls' interests often change over time, especially during their adolescent years. Rebecca and Emily enjoyed going on walks together, bonding over fashion, and working together on class work.

Rebecca felt pressured by her mother, which created a wedge in their relationship. She wondered if her mother cared more about her friend with whom she disagreed than Rebecca and her feelings. Rather than forcing Rebecca to make up with her friend and continue to spend time with her, her mother could have guided her to find a kind and direct way to sever the relationship. As adults, we need to do a better job of showing girls conflict is inevitable and healthy, and a lot can be learned if it's handled appropriately. Situations like these are a great opportunity to learn how to step away from hurtful relationships, whether it be for a few minutes, a few days, or a lifetime.

Another way we can help a girl to #BeSeen is by allowing her to express herself through her clothes. Culture can impact the way women and girls express themselves. For example, in some cultures, covering skin is a form of respect and modesty. In other cultures, showing a little more of the skin you're in can be an expression of confidence. Be conscious of the background of the girls you live and work with, as clothing choices can drastically differ, which is totally okay. Allow her to develop her own sense of style by choosing outfits on her own when shopping, getting dressed for school, or for an important function. If a girl is expected to wear a specific type of clothing due to her religious background or culture, there can still be freedoms in choosing things like the colors, styles, or accessories to make the outfit more suited for her.

Empowering girls to speak up, demonstrate their intelligence, and let their personalities shine are equally as important. For teachers, it is important to be mindful of who you call on in the classroom. Studies suggest boys receive more of their teacher's attention and are given more time to respond to questions. The book *Failing at Fairness: How America's Schools Cheat Girls* highlights findings from twenty years of research by two of America's most prominent social scientists. Their research findings suggested gender bias in our educational system creates a very different classroom experience for girls than for boys. Girls are often taught to defer to boys and to speak more quietly. They are usually given up to two-thirds less time than boys to speak in class.[33]

In addition to becoming aware of the aforementioned inequities, it is important to become conscious of the amount of time you allow students to think before responding. Even at a graduate level, I have heard more hesitant students suggest professors offer additional time between questions so they can process and have room to join the conversation when ready. (Note: Girls who speak the most don't necessarily

---

33 Myra Sadker and David Sadker, *Falling at Fairness* (New York: Touchstone, 1994).

have more confidence than girls who speak less frequently.) Sometimes, for all students to be seen and heard, we must be creative in the ways we invite students to express themselves. A few strategies may include using sticky notes, small-group discussions, or written reflections to cater to different types of learners and personalities.

One way I like to empower girls in my programming is switching leadership roles throughout the semester. Some girls are extremely eager to step into leadership while others are timider. When a girl needs a little boost, I'll pull her aside when no one else is watching and encourage her to be brave. I say something like, "I need help with X, and I thought of you, because (insert specific strength)…What do you think? Will you give it a try?" The key here is to highlight her strength and help her see why I chose her to be the leader.

This same technique can be used at home, especially if there are multiple siblings. For example, "Mom/Dad needs help with X. I know you're super talented at Y. Would you mind helping us out?" I always encourage parents to get some alone time with each child, if possible, so each child has individualized time to be seen and heard. I always loved when I had the opportunity to hang out with just my mom and dad without my three other siblings. It gave me a chance to share the things that were important in my life, helping me realize my value.

Another approach that can be especially helpful to being seen in a family setting is becoming aware of sibling dynamics. Is there one child who is more dominant or who gets ganged up on? How about one who never says much? While it's normal for siblings to have unique personalities, it is important to keep an eye out and take steps to empower children who may be more easily overlooked. If one sibling is being mistreated, help give that child or teen the words to stand up and speak out. It can be helpful to give an exact script for the child or teen to use.

One example from my own experience was observing a kindergartner named *Mary. Her second grade brother *Eric would frequently taunt her by entering her personal space. I showed her how to say, "Stop, I don't like it when you are in my space" to assert herself when she felt uncomfortable. I was constantly working with Eric to help him understand the first time someone says no, it means no.

His fifth grade sister *Michelle caught on to this lesson. It became so ingrained in her that when I made the mistake of not stopping something the first time, she called me out on it. I vividly remember her saying, "Hey, don't you always tell us that when somebody says stop it, it means the first time?" My light bulb lit up! This was the perfect time to model for her how to apologize and reinforce the importance of boundaries. I replied, "Yes, you are right. I am so sorry I didn't stop joking the first time. That was wrong of me, and I shouldn't have done that. I am proud of you for recognizing that it was wrong." This showed her I was serious about what I said and boundaries do matter.

It's important we teach girls to be assertive and stand up when they see something is wrong, just like Michelle did. We can teach them that rather than being passive or aggressive, they can assert themselves, standing up both for themselves and for others.

During a girls group I cotaught with a school counselor, we used the example of swings to teach about being assertive, passive, and aggressive.

Here are examples you can use to teach the girls the difference:

- Assertive: "I'd like a turn on the swing when you are finished."
- Passive: "Wow...you're lucky that you get to swing...I really wish I could..."
- Aggressive: "Get off the swing, now!"

While some progress has been made to expand mainstream conceptions of acceptable female bodies and behavior, messages of how girls should look, dress, act, and behave are still loud and clear. It is up to us to help girls decide whether or not these norms are comfortable and work for them. Some girls may want to dress up as princesses, while others may want to dress in baggy clothes and get dirty. Give her the freedom to choose, speak up, speak out, be heard, and ultimately #BeSeen.

KEY TAKEAWAYS
- Challenge your own gender biases.
- Give girls permission to express themselves and honor their boundaries.
- Teach girls how to be assertive. Sometimes this may mean giving them specific phrases to use.

Reflection: Think and reflect on two to three areas where my own struggles or biases impact my ability to allow her to #BeSeen. How can I work to eliminate these?

_____

_____

_____

_____

_____

_____

_____

_____

_____

_____

_____

_____

_____

CHAPTER 13

#SPORTS&FITNESS

———

Coming from a background in exercise science, I've always believed physical activity, fitness, and sports can positively impact the way a girl feels about herself. Physical activity and fitness can include lifting weights, dancing, martial arts, running, hiking, and biking. This chapter focuses on the benefits of sports and fitness; however, it is important to note competition and wellness can take unhealthy forms, leading to an excessive focus on appearance, perfectionism, and toxic comparison. Overall, this chapter will focus on the positive aspects of what sports and fitness can do for a young girl and her self-esteem.

Research has shown a variety of sports and increased physical activity can greatly influence the way girls feel about themselves. The Girl's Index reported, "Girls who play sports report higher levels of confidence at all ages. Girls experience a significant drop in confidence throughout middle school, however, girls who play sports report confidence at consistently higher rates...[They] have higher opinions of their abilities and competencies." In fact, there was a 38 percent difference between girls who did not play sports and those who did play sports in their perception of being "not good at lots of things."[34]

Just because girls are involved in sports and fitness does not mean their confidence will not decline during this challenging time we call adolescence. However, the more protective factors we can put into place for helping our young women, the less likely it is we will see such drastic declines in rates of confidence.

This is why at Empowered & Poised we strive to ensure girls learn not only how to be mentally and socially fit, but also physically fit. It isn't about "losing weight" or "looking better," it's about treating your body with respect. Respecting yourself enough to set goals, stick to them, and have a growth mind-set. In other words, rather than saying you can't do something, say I can't do it *yet.*

The Sport Journal published a great piece regarding the impact of sports on a girl's self-esteem and confidence. It reminded us, "As girls move from grade school to high school, they drop out of sports at a rate six times higher than boys." This leads us to question, does the impact of declining rates of participation in sport correlate with the drop we see in girls' confidence? Sports and fitness can help girls realize what their bodies can do, as opposed to how their bodies should look. *The Sport Journal* said girls are essentially learning to develop "physical competence." Girls learn to have control of their bodies while depending on the skills they've gained

---

34 Lisa Hinkelman, *The Girls' Index: Girls and Sports Impact Report* (Columbus: Ruling Our eXperiences, Inc, 2018), 3.

through practice. Girls learn how to become their own advocates or "personal cheerleaders," encouraging themselves toward possibilities and accomplishments.[35]

In addition, sports create an environment where girls can learn to honor their bodies, build resilience, and foster meaningful relationships with their coaches and teammates. Fitness can help lift a girl's mood because of the rush of endorphins she gets when exercising. I have found the gym and walks in nature help me calm my mind when it gets too busy from everything going on in my life.

Learning boxing during my adolescent years was also extremely empowering. I didn't fight in the ring. Nevertheless, it encouraged me to push myself to new limits, both physically and mentally. When I was boxing consistently, I felt unstoppable. I found a new sense of power within myself. I felt strong and capable. The world of fitness also became a place where I developed socially. I have met so many supportive people through the fitness world. In group fitness classes, it is common to see individuals cheering one another on, moving together, and embracing each other's unique talents.

We can be those people for girls—the people who back them up, stand by their side, and provide them with encouragement. We must also help girls focus on unearthing their own unique gifts and talents. Some girls are good at arts while others are talented in sports or academics. As mentioned

---

35 Allison Schultz, "You Go Girl! The Link between Girls' Positive Self-Esteem and Sports," *The Sport Journal* 2, no. 2 (1999): 1–3.

in the #Exposure chapter, we can help girls uncover their passions and talents through exposure to a variety of people, places, and activities.

One of the women I met throughout my own fitness journey is Melissa Heaverlo. Melissa, a Hispanic fitness guru, shared about her adolescent experience. Growing up, she was the only Latina in her core group of friends. Oftentimes, she was left out. They'd go to the mall, movies, and on other adventures and didn't invite her. Of course, this didn't make her feel great. In an attempt to protect herself and her feelings, she would make up a bunch of excuses why she wasn't invited. Eventually, she decided to ask her best friend Allie why she was never invited. Allie told her it was because she was "always broke." Having a single, Latina mom, Melissa and her family didn't always have the luxury of having extra money to spend on nonessentials. After hearing this, Melissa was devastated but worked to move forward, acting like nothing was wrong. She continued trying hard to fit in.

In addition to being left out by her "friends," she was bullied by her classmates. Growing up in the desert in Arizona, her skin was dark. As early as kindergarten, she was called names and teased because of her dark skin and features. She began to think she needed to lose weight and stay inside so her skin didn't darken. Melissa grew up in a period where media wasn't quite as prevalent. So, she didn't begin comparing herself to others until her classmates pointed out characteristics that were deemed as "not as good." At one point in her young life, the bullying got so bad she had to have an adult walk her from class to class to make sure she was safe.

As a release from her painful feelings and thoughts, Melissa turned to dance. She and her Latinx friends found peace and solace in this space. While Melissa didn't always feel like she was the smartest, she was confident in her abilities to move. She felt fully comfortable in her own skin through dancing. She loved the way it felt to practice hard and have the routines she was dedicated to come together. Therefore, she got involved in anything and everything she could that was performance-related. She joined cheer, pom, and dance teams as a way to express herself. She also began lifting weights, which helped her feel strong and confident.

Years later, as an adult, Melissa made it a goal to help other people love the skin they were in. She did this through creating Mob-Deep. This group combines her passion for dance and mixed martial arts. Still today, she is grateful for the "mob" of people supporting her on her fitness journey. She feels "stronger in a pack than standing on [her] own." She didn't want others' self-esteem to plummet the way hers did because of the constant bullying she faced growing up. "There are people out there who will back you up, stand by your side, and not just tell you that you're not going to make it because of your skin color."

Another athlete of great influence who overcame criticism is American soccer player Megan Rapinoe, who was on multiple World Cup–winning teams. After winning the World Cup, she posted a video where she stated, "I deserve this," as she was parading along holding the trophy. Coach Christen, who works with Olympic swimmers on building confidence, shared this post on her Instagram because she was stoked about this win and how much Megan and her team *did* deserve this win. Sadly, she had to turn off the post's comments because of how horrifying some of the comments from other women were. They said things like "She's so disgusting...so cocky...She needs to humble herself." Coach Christen found this devastating because she believes all too often girls are shamed into "stepping out of their light." Girls should not be called "cocky" when they are proud of their hard work, skills, and accomplishments.

Confidence coach Christen shared some other interesting insights with me as well. She said with many of the athletes she works with, the biggest barrier holding them back is fear. At times, their fear can be so strong it can be paralyzing. They question, "What if I don't deserve it?" with "it" referring to succeeding, being prepared, or placing at their meets. Rarely, if ever, when a "What if...?" creeps in does she see it being something positive like "What if I beat my record, place, or do well?" It's much more often "What if I fail?" She encourages girls to go back to their "home base" and "their truth."

A two-time Olympian she worked with, *Molly, opened up to her about what was holding her back—fear and a current lack of motivation. Just like with confidence, levels of motivation can ebb and flow, even for the most talented athletes and most confident girls. Low motivation often stems from discouragement rather than laziness. This was the case with Molly. Coach Christen encouraged Molly to circle back to her home base and find her truth.

A confidence journal is a tool Coach Christen uses to help her athletes recognize their accomplishments. As mentioned in the #Affirmation chapter, girls don't buy into affirmations that don't align with their beliefs. The journal gives girls the opportunity to list out, concretely and visibly, their accomplishments. This allows them to own their truth through the use of self-affirmations. Girls write about things like the hard work they've put into practicing. They state the facts, reminding themselves why they are capable.

Molly became focused on her perceived weaknesses as a swimmer, and she began to see herself as incapable in other areas too. She struggled to complete her confidence journals consistently and viewed her missing assignments as further evidence of her inadequacy. Coach Christen knew Molly needed some successes, however small, to begin rebuilding her confidence.

Molly was also able to look back at her journal to help put to rest some of the "What if...?" questions. Ultimately, this translated into confidence in her swimming. Coach Christen highlighted when we consistently give ourselves credit for small accomplishments, it can lead to believing in our abilities.

Too often, our "What ifs" in sports and in life are focused on comparison. "What if I'm not the best?" "What if I fail?" I have to admit, when I first started Empowered & Poised, I had a lot of those negative "What ifs" running through my mind. "What if my program isn't as good as the other programs out there?" "What if people don't take me seriously because of my age?"

I quickly realized it doesn't have to be about competition. As humans, we are stronger when we come together and collaborate with one another, bringing our unique talents to the table. I had the fortune of conducting programming in a local public school district. The school district offered five other girls groups. While the overarching goals of the programs were the same, each one of us had a unique approach. There is space at the table for everyone. We need to teach girls, both in sports and in life, we are stronger when we do two things: work together and embrace who we are.

For this reason, I want to highlight another organization local to the Cleveland area, where I grew up: Girls with Sole. Girls with Sole is run by Liz Ferro, a white woman who recognizes the importance of helping girls step outside their comfort zones and try new activities, especially involving movement. Over many years, Liz witnessed girls saying, "We don't do that," when asked to try a new activity such as hiking or paddle boarding. When they said "we," they were referring to people of their racial and ethnic backgrounds. They lacked exposure to these activities as well as access to media and role models who looked like them accomplishing these activities. Therefore, saying "We don't do that" protected them from displaying their fear and lack of confidence when it came to fitness.

Time and time again, Liz would see girls' confidence increase as they learned they were capable and they weren't "too this" or "too that." For many of the girls she works with, "it seems impossible, until it's done." When the girls in her program realize they are capable, they become overwhelmed with a sense of childlike joy. She often sees them running up and down the hills they thought they could not even walk. They call out to her, "I did it, look at me!"

She shared one of the most incredible stories with me about the impact fitness can have on a girl's view of herself. Liz met a fourteen-year-old named *Mia at a residential treatment center. Mia was kept in restraints nearly half the day due to severe behavioral issues. She refused to participate in Girls with Sole because she hated exercising. One day, Mia decided to go to the program. After a couple sessions, she realized she loved it. She enjoyed it so much she wanted to run a marathon (literally)!

However, she faced a challenge. She was bulimic. Bulimia nervosa is an eating disorder that involves eating large amounts of food followed by purging (intentionally vomiting the food). Liz agreed to help Mia, but let her know if she wanted to run a marathon, she would need to keep in food to fuel her through it. Mia took it upon herself to develop a visual aid with healthy images and pictures of people who supported her to keep on the top of the toilet seat. This helped her remember every time she wanted to purge she had a goal for herself to keep going and keep training. By the time Mia turned sixteen, she completed a duathlon, a sprint triathlon, and her first marathon with Liz alongside her! She was also able to move into a transitional living program, where she had more freedom.

Girls like Mia saying "We don't do that" reflects just a small portion of the inequities that impact girls within sport. In 2018, the Tucker Center for Research on Girls & Women in Sport reported, "The increase in sport-based positive youth development programs means that girls are learning about Lerner's 5Cs through physical activity–competence, character, confidence, connection, and caring. But unfortunately, very few sports programs are gender sensitive or take into account how systemic sexism, poverty, racism...and experiences of abuse shape girls' lives...Without awareness of these contextual factors, sport and physical activity programs limit the good they can provide to all girls."[36]

Mia's story illustrates just how powerful physical activity can be in the development of confidence for all girls, especially if they've never been exposed before. Movement can help connect people with supportive others and with their own power. Fitness can help individuals move from fearful to fully alive.

No one is fearless, not even the most confident girl in the world.

—COACH CHRISTEN

Fear and "What ifs" can creep in for anyone. As athletes, girls must learn how to enter a competition, whether it be in sport, in fitness, or with themselves, and know fear is going to be part of the battle. However, when a girl is prepared and knows this completely normal fear is going to arise, she can learn and build skills to feel more prepared. Then, as Coach Christen says, "confidence can flow" freely.

---

36 Tucker Center for Research on Girls & Women in Sport, *The 2018 Tucker Center Research Report Developing Physically Active Girls: An Evidence-Based Multidisciplinary Approach* (University of Minnesota, Minneapolis, MN: Tucker Center for Research on Girls & Women in Sport, 2018), 65.

CHAPTER 14

HOW TO: SPORTS & FITNESS

My education and experiences have taught me the importance of physical activity for not only our physical well-being, but for our overall wellness, including social and mental well-being. According to the Centers for Disease Control and Prevention, "Regular physical activity is one of the most important things you can do for your health. Everyone can experience the health benefits of physical activity—age, abilities, ethnicity, shape, or size do not matter."[37] Fitness can help reduce risk for disease, strengthen bones and muscles, and improve overall quality of life. The earlier we can get girls involved in physical activity, the better!

During childhood, my parents exposed me to a variety of physical activity outlets, including soccer, softball, dance, hiking, biking, skating, basketball, and swimming. To this

---

37 "Benefits of Physical Activity," Centers for Disease Control and Prevention, accessed February 8, 2021.

day, I still love biking, hiking, and dancing. As previously mentioned, the activities to which we expose girls at a young age can greatly impact their future interests. Additionally, research suggests there is "a positive relationship between sports participation and pro-social behavior, subjective health, well-being, and [a] sense of coherence. Coherence reflects a person's ability to cope with stressful events in a health-promoting way."[38]

As I moved into adolescence, I explored some other options: volleyball and cheerleading. I remember attending one basketball practice and wasn't excited about it. Even though all the other girls in my class were playing on the team, my parents never pressured me to participate in activities that weren't of interest to me. I appreciated having the power of choice when it came to how I wanted to move and stay active.

It wasn't until late in my high school career I developed a true passion for fitness. In fact, in the beginning of high school, it would be a rare occasion to find me lifting, running, or doing anything where I had to exert too much physical effort. One of the motivators for me getting into lifting was my high school fitness class elective, where I learned how to lift.

Now, when working with girls through Empowered & Poised, I like to develop fun activities to get them moving and trying new types of exercise. One great activity that works for

---

38 Sabina Super et al., "Examining the Relationship between Sports Participation and Youth Developmental Outcomes for Socially Vulnerable Youth," *BMC Public Health* 18, no. 1012 (2018): 1–12.

women and girls of all ages is developing a workout challenge. To do this, choose roughly ten exercises and write them down on a piece of paper. These movements can include jumping jacks, planks, wall sits, push-ups, running in place, or any other exercises that get you moving. From here, specify how long or how many of each exercise will be completed. For example, you may write "Do twenty-five jumping jacks" or "Hold a plank for one minute." Then, encourage the individual or group you are working with to complete the entire challenge. To make it more challenging and fun, you can increase the number of times it needs to be completed, put on music, or make it a friendly competition. It is important to take a girl's current physical activity level and skill into account.

Introducing sports or activities you liked growing up to the girls in your life is okay, but don't pressure her to become a star athlete in a sport she doesn't enjoy to recreate your own childhood.

Be gentle with girls as they are still developing their own interests. New fitness interests can be developed all the way through adulthood. Never stop exploring new ways you and the girls you support can get and stay active! You can join the local fitness club, explore ways to stay active outdoors, or take advantage of online fitness classes. YouTube has a plethora of family-friendly workout classes that can be found through a simple search of "at-home workouts."

Fitness is also a great way to bring the family together and set goals. You can work toward accomplishing a 5k or even a marathon together. You can try out a new fitness activity like rock climbing, yoga, or kayaking. You can also make it a goal to integrate activity into your lifestyle by taking a walk after dinner, stretching during commercials, or going for bike rides on the weekends.

When developing goals, make sure that they are SMART. This means they are: specific, measurable, attainable, relevant, and timely. Once you come up with the goal, write it down.

Here's an example: Train together as a family to complete the local 5k Turkey Trot that takes place on November 26 this year to achieve your first ever race and move toward a healthier lifestyle as a family.

S–It is specific because it involves **who** is participating, **what** the goal is, **when** it is taking place, **where** it will be, and **why** the goal is important.
M–It is measurable because it will either be completed or will not.
A–It is achievable because you are not jumping from being new runners or walkers into an entire marathon.
R–It is relevant because the goal is to get more active as a family, and success breeds success.
T–It is timely/time-oriented because there is a date associated with the goal: November 26.

We can teach the girls we work or live with how to develop SMART goals for fitness, as well as in other areas of their lives. Accomplishing goals is a definite confidence booster!

One goal I set for myself was starting an organization on my college campus. I called the organization H.O.P.E. (Helping Others Participate in Exercise). This organization encouraged individuals to stay socially, mentally, and physically fit, just like in Empowered & Poised. Individuals who were not typically interested in or involved in fitness had the opportunity to try atypical fitness activities. A few examples of areas we explored were Bikram yoga, barre, Sky Zone's jump class, boxing, and boot camp. I had to persevere to keep the organization running while juggling my school and work obligations. It was not always easy, but I learned so much from this leadership experience and continued to build my own resilience. Sports and fitness can teach us how to fall and gracefully get back up.

Keep in mind there is a difference between helping young people "tough it out" when things get challenging and forcing them into doing something they just don't like. For this reason, it is critical when encouraging the girls in your life to get involved with sports and fitness, you don't pressure them into continuing an activity they clearly don't enjoy. Allow them to try a variety of activities, and ideally one or two should stick and can become part of their routine! When a girl builds skills and is healthy in all areas of life, she is much more likely to be confident.

KEY TAKEAWAYS_
- Exposure to a variety of activities is important.
- Be creative about the ways you help girls get involved with fitness. Sports are a great go-to, but they aren't for everyone, and that's okay.

- Remember, a girl's background may play a role in what she thinks she can and cannot do. Therefore, we must approach sports and fitness from the lens of conscious empowerment similar to all other areas explored in this book.

Reflection: In what ways can I encourage physical activity? List as many activities as you can, and share the list with the girl(s) in your life. Highlight the activities she's interested in, and give them a try!

_____

_____

_____

_____

_____

_____

_____

_____

_____

_____

_____

_____

CHAPTER 15

FINAL THOUGHTS

"I raise up my voice—not so I can shout but so that those without a voice can be heard…we cannot succeed when half of us are held back," said Malala Yousafzai, Pakistani activist for female education and the youngest Nobel Prize laureate. This quote clearly portrays my reason for starting Empowered & Poised and writing this book. As a woman with more blessings than I can count, I can only hope the messages shared in this book positively impact your life and the girls you love. My prayer is girls from all backgrounds can feel seen and heard and know they are valued. There is no right or wrong way to be confident, as confidence comes in all shapes and sizes, just like girls. Stephanie Hull said it best when she said, "There are many, many ways to be self-confident…Find yourself [and] be true to that person!"

Take the wisdom from this book that works for you and the girls in your life, and leave what doesn't serve you. The information shared is not meant to dictate hard rules, but to offer principles to guide you in helping girls navigate this challenging world.

As one of my graduate professors, Amy Korsch-Williams, once shared, "I think that we can promote confidence within each other...We must rally around our children and build community. Women talking openly with each other, building relationships, and building each other up, not tearing one another down, goes a long way."

Remember to #BeThatAdult all girls need in their lives, #Affirm girls and teach them how to self-affirm, #Expose them to new opportunities that broaden their horizons, work toward #Representation of all young women, encourage girls to #BeSeen, embrace their authenticity, and work towards maintaining a healthy lifestyle with a dose of #Sports&Fitness. If we make mistakes along the way, it's okay!

Take the stories you have read, the organizations and individuals you have learned about, and the information you have gleaned, and continue to press forward. Informing ourselves is only the first step. Our time, attention, and support are what makes the difference to girls.

While it is clear we still have a long way to go to ensure girls are all raised in a consciously Empowered way, we stand on the shoulders of the women who have come before us. Thank you to our mentors, our mothers, our teachers, our coaches, and all others who stand with us and fight for us. Thank you to everyone who has taken the time to read this book with hopes of helping our future generations be strong, confident, self-assured, consciously Empowered women.

Reflection: What is the greatest takeaway from this book? How can I implement three of the lessons I have learned throughout this book to my own life?

_____

_____

_____

_____

_____

_____

_____

_____

_____

_____

_____

_____

ACKNOWLEDGMENTS

I'd like to start by thanking the Lord for this opportunity and blessing. Without His strength, it would have not been possible to get through writing a book, making my way through graduate school, running a business, and doing all the other things I do.

Thank you to everyone who has been a part of my journey in writing *Conscious Empowerment.* I am extremely grateful for the outpouring of support and encouragement.

Thank you to my family and friends for walking by my side. I love you all very much!

A special thank-you to my significant other, Michael Alexander-Leeks, for being my rock throughout this journey, letting me cry on your shoulder, helping calm my worries, and reading through my many drafts. Your hours of editing my school papers helped me gain enough confidence in my writing abilities to take on this project. I love you.

Thank you to Thaiger Adanoldo for assisting me with my promo video, and to Matt Radicelli for helping me produce pop-up and live video events to promote the prelaunch. You guys rock!

Thanks to everyone who has been a part of the Empowered & Poised mission and movement, including my wonderful team of interns. Thank you to Michaela Toth for stepping up in your role to help lighten my load. Shout-out to the JCU entrepreneurship department! I truly could not do this without all of you. I wish you all success and good fortune in your life. May you always remember to "Be you. Be strong. Be Empowered & Poised."

Thank you to all of the individuals who have featured me and my book in your blogs, podcasts, and other media platforms to help me share the *Conscious Empowerment* message and empower girls from all around the world.

Thanks to everyone who provided feedback on early drafts, especially my primary beta readers:

Amy Williams, CSEP
Michael Alexander-Leeks
Meredith Ellis, MEd
Natalie Siston, author of *Let Her Out: Reclaim Who You Have Always Been*

Thanks to everyone who preordered a copy of my book and donated to my prelaunch campaign. This was one of the most challenging parts of the book-writing process. You all helped to remind me there are many people in my communities who love me and believe in my hopes and dreams.

Names are in alphabetical order by first name.

Abigail Chauvin
Abigail Migdal
Alex Michaels
Alysha Ellis
Amit Maranganti
Andrea Pollock
Angela Magnes
Anika Prots
Anne Glorioso*
Anne Cloud
Anthony Surace
Ashley Parker
Aurelia Mino
Ayesha Rehman
Ben Allison*
Benjamin Bard*
Beth Fink
Bo Smith
Brian McNair
Brionna Burgos
Brittney Seale
Bryan Putka
Cali Cheminant
Caroline Bard*
Chris Keller
Chris Ruma-Cullen
Christina Iafelice

Christine Varricchio
Ciara Adkins/Anna Reed
Cindy Svonavec
Clair Dabernig
Clarissa Russell
Darian Berdysz
Debii McAllister
Deirdre Krul
Doan Winkel
Douglas Jones
Edie Fiala
Eleanor Bergholz
Ellie Reed
Elliot Golias*
Emily Papesh
Emily Augustine
Eric Eickoff
Evan Cooper
Genevieve Miller
Gianna Uson
Gloria Ware
Greg Farnell*
Heather Horschler
Heidi Asplin
Hina Tariq
Illene Frankel
Jared Marks*

Jay Apple
Jeanette Livingston
Jeff Hexter
Jeremy Rich
Jill Banner*
Jill Frankfort
Jill Snyder*
John Vlach
Julia Ruggerio
Kamron Khan
Kat Caya
Kathryn Ross
Kathy & Tom Futey
Kayla O'Brien
Kelli McCorvey
Kelly Biggar*
Kim Allamby*
Laura Majkrzak
Laura Hayes
Lee Paiva
Linda Miletti
Linda & Daniel Berdysz*
Lindsey Berdysz*
Lisa Witherite
Lucy Whichelo
Madeline Coburn*
Mai Segawa
Maneke Snowden
Maria Jeancola
Mariana Edelman
Marika Reisberg
Marivi Howell-Arza

Mary DeVille
Mary Ann Hexter
Massiel Valenzuela
Matt Radicelli
Mattia Robles
Megan Putka
Melanie Flowers
Melissa Thompson
Meredith Hillman
Michelle Bransky*
Michelle Shlachter
Mo McKenna
Molly Haaga*
Monique Sacks
Nancy Neuer*
Natalie Siston*
Nathalie Rudledge
Nina Rossi
Olivia Biss
Pamela Gray-Mason
Patty Chamoun
Pauline Schlotter
Pollyn Horvath
Rachel Czerny
Rachel Miller
Rebecca Herr
Rebecca Ruppert McMahon*
Rebecca Joseph
Robin Eisen
Ruth Drab
Ruth Reed*
Ryan Konikoff*

Samantha Carroll-Syracuse	Stephanie Burgess
Sandra Alexander	Summer Haggins
Sandra Slater*	Susan Bard*
Sandy Chauvin	Tiffany Lewis
Sandy Longo	Toby & Melanie Maloney*
Sarah Balzer	Todd Goldstein
Sarah Andrews	Tom Bonda
Sarah Radcliff	Tommy Murtaugh
Shante Roddy*	Tyrell Davis
Sheila Long	Vanessa Moreno
Sheri Stevens	Vivian Copley
Sheryl Matney	Wendy Chaney
Sonya Paster	Yang Li

* Additional donation or multiple copies purchased

I'd also like to thank Eric Koester, Brian Bies, Melody Delgado Lorbeer, Kristy Elam, Gjorgji Pejkovski, Morgan Rohde, Amanda Brown, Mateusz Cichosz, Mary Hanna, and the rest of the Creator Institute and New Degree Press individuals I've had the honor to work alongside. Thank you for helping my vision come to life and answering my many questions along the way!

Thank you, Gracias, Merci, Xièxie, Salamat, Arigatō, Cảm ơn, Toda, Dziękuję ci, Gamsahabnida, Shukran, Danke, Asante, Jee shukriya, and many more thanks to all!

APPENDIX

INTRODUCTION

Gowland, Lelia. "How Your Racial and Gender Identities Can Overlap and Affect Your Career." *Forbes*, June 27, 2018. https://www.forbes.com/sites/leliagowland/2018/06/27/how-your-overlapping-identities-can-affect-your-career/?sh=1e7245b45a38.

Hinkelman, Lisa. *The Girls' Index: New Insights into the Complex World of Today's Girls.* Columbus: Ruling Our eXperiences, Inc., 2017.

CHAPTER 1

Women, UN. "Intersectional Feminism: What It Means and Why It Matters Right Now," Medium, July 1, 2020. https://un-women.medium.com/intersectional-feminism-what-it-means-and-why-it-matters-right-now-7743bfa16757.

StrategyOne and Ann Kearney-Cooke. *Real Girls, Real Pressure: A National Report on the State of Self-Esteem.* New York City, NY: American Association of University Women, 2008.

CHAPTER 2

Burton, Neel. "Self-Confidence versus Self-Esteem." *Psychology Today.* Sussex Publishers, October 19, 2015. https://www.psychologytoday.com/us/blog/hide-and-seek/201510/self-confidence-versus-self-esteem?amp.

Fernstrom, Madelyn. "Dr. Fernstrom: Self-Esteem vs. Self-Confidence—and How to Boost Both!" *NBCNews.com.* NBCUniversal News Group, May 24, 2019. https://www.nbcnews.com/know-your-value/feature/dr-fernstrom-self-esteem-vs-self-confidence-how-boost-both-ncna1008986.

Garey, Juliann. "Raising Girls with Healthy Self-Esteem." *Child Mind Institute,* July 28, 2020. https://childmind.org/article/raising-girls-with-healthy-self-esteem/.

Herzfeld, Stephanie. "New Social Experiment by Always® Reveals Harmful Impact Commonly Used Phrase Has on Girls." *Procter & Gamble.* Updated December 2, 2020. https://news.pg.com/news-releases/news-details/2014/New-Social-Experiment-by-Always-Reveals-Harmful-Impact-Commonly-Used-Phrase-has-on-Girls/default.aspx.

Hinkelman, Lisa. & Sibyl West. *Girls, Diversity & the Future: A Girls' Index Impact Report.* The Girls' Index. Columbus: Ruling Our eXperiences, Inc., 2020.

CHAPTER 3

Hinkelman, Lisa. *The Girls' Index: New Insights into the Complex World of Today's Girls.* Columbus: Ruling Our eXperiences, Inc, 2017.

Roehlkepartain, Eugene, Kent Pekel, Amy Syvertsen, Jenna Sethi, Theresa Sullivan, and Peter Scales. *Relationships First: Creating Connections that Help Young People Thrive*. Minneapolis, MN: Search Institute, January 19, 2018. https://www.search-institute. org/new-research-report/.

StrategyOne and Ann Kearney-Cooke. *Real Girls, Real Pressure: A National Report on the State of Self-Esteem*. New York City, NY: American Association of University Women, 2008.

CHAPTER 4

Almendrala, Anna. "5 Signs You Were Raised by Helicopter Parents." *HuffPost* (blog). Updated March 14, 2021. https://www. huffpost.com/entry/5-ways-to-tell-you-were-raised-by-helicopter-parents_n_5609de6ee4b0dd850308e260.

CHAPTER 5

Girls Inc. "Home Page." Accessed March 20, 2021. https://www. girlsinctnv.org/

CHAPTER 6

Obama, Michelle. "Remarks by Mrs. Obama and Madam Kim of the Republic of Korea at a Cultural Event at Annandale High School in Annandale, Virginia." *The American Presidency Project*, October 13, 2011. https://www.presidency.ucsb. edu/documents/remarks-mrs-obama-and-madam-kim-the-republic-korea-cultural-event-annandale-high-school.

USAID. "Let Girls Learn." *US Agency for International Development.* Updated January 26, 2017. https://www.usaid.gov/letgirlslearn/fact-sheet.

CHAPTER 7

Warner, Judith, Nora Ellmann, and Diana Boesch. "The Women's Leadership Gap." *Center for American Progress,* November 20 2018, www.americanprogress.org/issues/women/reports/2018/11/20/461273/womensleadership-gap-2/.

Wong, Frieda, and Richard Halgin. "The 'Model Minority': Bane or Blessing for Asian Americans?" *Journal of Multicultural Counseling and Development* 34, no. 1 (January 2006): 38–49. doi:10.1002/j.2161-1912.2006.tb00025.x.

CHAPTER 8

Gilligan, Carol. *Mapping the Moral Domain: A Contribution of Women's Thinking to Psychological Theory and Education* (Center for the Study of Gender, Education and Human Development, Harvard University Graduate School of Education, 1988).

MediaSmarts. "Media and Girls." August 22, 2014. mediasmarts.ca/gender-representation/women-and-girls/media-and-girls.

CHAPTER 9

Annenberg School for Communication. "Study Reveals the Neural Mechanics of Self-Affirmation." November 20, 2015, www.asc.upenn.edu/news-events/news/study-reveals-neural-mechanics-self-affirmation.

Berwick, Carly. "Keeping Girls in STEM: 3 Barriers, 3 Solutions." Edutopia, George Lucas Educational Foundation, March 12, 2019, www.edutopia.org/article/keeping-girls-stem-3-barriers-3solutions.

Cohen, Geoffrey, and David K. Sherman. "The Psychology of Change: Self-Affirmation and Social Psychological Intervention." *Annual Review of Psychology* 65, no. 1(2014): 333–71.

Encyclopedia of Adolescence, s.v., "Affirmation," by Roger J.R. Levesque, February 28, 2018, https://doi.org/10.1007/978-3-319-33228-4_755.

Moore, Catherine. "Positive Daily Affirmations: Is There Science Behind It?" PositivePsychology.com, January 30, 2021, positivepsychology.com/daily-affirmations/.

CHAPTER 10

Johnson, Norine. "On Treating Adolescent Girls: Focus on Strengths and Resiliency in Psychotherapy." *Journal of Clinical Psychology*, 59, no. 11 (November 2003): 1194.

CHAPTER 11

Mahalik, James R., Elisabeth B. Morray, Aimée Coonerty-Femiano, Larry H. Ludlow, Suzanne M. Slattery, and Andrew Smiler. "Development of the Conformity to Feminine Norms Inventory." *Sex Roles* 52, no. 7 (April 2005): 417–435. https://doi.org/10.1007/s11199-005-3709-7.

No Means No Worldwide. "About." Accessed February 7, 2021. https://www.nomeansnoworldwide.org/our-story.

CHAPTER 12

Brown, Brené. *Daring Greatly: How the Courage to Be Vulnerable Transforms the Way We Live, Love, Parent, and Lead*. London, UK: Penguin Random House Audio Publishing Group, 2011.

Sadker, Myra, and David Sadker. *Falling at Fairness*. New York: Touchstone, 1994.

CHAPTER 13

Hinkelman, Lisa. *The Girls' Index: Girls and Sports Impact Report*. Columbus: Ruling Our eXperiences, Inc, 2018.

Schultz, Allison. "You Go Girl! the Link between Girls' Positive Self-Esteem and Sports." *The Sport Journal* 2, no. 2 (1999): 1–3.

Tucker Center for Research on Girls & Women in Sport. *The 2018 Tucker Center Research Report Developing Physically Active Girls: An Evidence-Based Multidisciplinary Approach*. University of Minnesota, Minneapolis, MN: Tucker Center for Research on Girls & Women in Sport, 2018.

CHAPTER 14

Centers for Disease Control and Prevention. "Benefits of Physical Activity." Accessed February 8, 2021, https://www.cdc.gov/physicalactivity/basics/pa-health/index.htm.

Super, Sabina, Niels Hermens, Kirsten Verkooijen, and Maria Koelen. "Examining the Relationship between Sports Participation and Youth Developmental Outcomes for Socially Vulnerable Youth." *BMC Public Health* 18, no. 1012 (2018): 1–12. https://doi.org/10.1186/s12889-018-5955-y.

Made in the USA
Monee, IL
12 July 2021